Halsey William Wilson

The H. W. Wilson Company

HALF A CENTURY

OF BIBLIOGRAPHIC PUBLISHING

BY

John Lawler

UNIVERSITY OF MINNESOTA PRESS, Minneapolis

LONDON · GEOFFREY CUMBERLEGE · OXFORD UNIVERSITY PRESS

Foreword

One often wonders what librarianship would be like today if there had never been an H. W. Wilson Company. Or take scholarship in general, the dissemination of ideas and information through printed materials. What would it be like today if there had never been a *Cumulative Book Index*, a *Readers' Guide to Periodical Literature*, or an *Agricultural Index* — to mention only a few of the many significant aids which are now so much a part of the everyday life of libraries and scholarship that they are more or less taken for granted?

Of course, men have to have ideas and record them. Other men must assemble knowledge and record it. Still other men must interpret and analyze knowledge and record their conclusions. All this work must be recorded if it is to have any value for society. And in these days of rotary printing presses, of linotype machines, of printing by photo-offset processes, so much knowledge, so much information, has been and is being recorded that society is literally swamped by the printed word.

The unsung heroes of scholarship today are the various agencies of bibliography — the locaters, identifiers, indexers of materials. For without indexes and controls to locate material, the student and the scholar would be helpless. Libraries are certainly one of the most important of these agencies, but if any one name had to be chosen as most outstanding, that name undoubtedly would be Halsey W. Wilson and his H. W. Wilson Company.

Mr. Lawler's excellent book is more than the record of a man, a company, and the loyal members of that company. It is the story of an idea, a service, a contribution to librarianship and scholarship. That contribution can never be completely isolated and measured, for it has played a vital though unspectacular part in nearly every scholarly activity of the past half-century.

E. W. McDiarmid

LIBRARIAN, UNIVERSITY OF MINNESOTA

Minneapolis, Minnesota
February 12, 1950

Table of Contents

Appendixes

Illustrations between pages 90 and 91

The H. W. Wilson Company

Prologue

On the east bank of the Harlem River, which separates the island of Manhattan from the borough of the Bronx, stands a row of three connected buildings midway between two famed institutions: Yankee Stadium and the Polo Grounds.

The curious visitor may be startled by the thirty-foot lighthouse atop the tallest of these structures. Consulting a map of the city, he will learn that ocean-going vessels could not .approach within several miles of the site; and no one will have to inform him that the small craft on the well-lighted river do not need such navigational aids.

The mystery is readily solved.

The lighthouse has no functional purpose. It is the trademark of the firm whose name appears emblazoned across the central building: the H. W. Wilson Company, the world's largest publisher of bibliographic tools. According to a favorite company phrase, it symbolizes the way in which the company's indexes "enlighten a path through the maze of books and periodicals."

Wandering into the plant in search of further knowledge, the visitor may be even more puzzled.

The thunder of huge presses is deafening on one floor; the silence on another is rather intimidating. The printing department is an almost exclusively male world; the editorial offices resemble large classrooms in a girls' school. The absence of floor-to-ceiling partitions creates a strange impression — only emphasized by the head-tall bookcases which surround each section to form a bewildering crisscross of dark corridors. Books and magazines are scattered everywhere: in stacks, shelves, hallways, and stairs, on desks, counters, window sills, and chairs. They are like the creeping undergrowth of a jungle, forever advancing despite the best efforts to control them.

If he wishes, the visitor can collect a mass of statistics which, in all likelihood, will increase his confusion.

Every year some thirty thousand books, twenty thousand periodicals, and a countless number of pamphlets arrive in the mail to be analyzed, classified, and listed in one or more of the company's two dozen major indexes and catalogs. . . .

This work requires a staff of three hundred and seventy people on an annual payroll of more than three quarters of a million dollars. . . .

About forty-five thousand libraries, business firms, and individuals pay one and a half million dollars annually for the company's services. Almost two thousand of these are located in sixty-four foreign nations, ranging from Afghanistan to Switzerland, from Wales to Iraq, from Ireland to Palestine, from Africa to Siam. . . .

The company's monthly postage bill is some four thousand dollars. . . .

The periodical supply department carries more than three million copies of back-number magazines for sale. . . .

Almost two thousand . . .

But before collapsing under the weight of these figures, the visitor should meet Halsey W. Wilson, the president of the company, at his massive roll-top desk in a corner of the fourth floor. A national magazine once remarked that he looked "just as a bibliographer ought to look." This cryptic observation may be revealing; but he can be more precisely described as a ruddy, round-faced man dressed in a dark suit and ankle-high black shoes. He has a baldish head, with a friar's fringe of white hair at the sides and back. Though ordinarily serious in manner, he is rarely solemn; and even his rimless spectacles cannot obscure an occasional twinkle, which friends recognize as a warning signal that he is about to utter a pun or relate an anecdote.

The cavernous desk is another clue to his character. It has an appearance of complete disorder; yet, by exercising an impressive memory or by using an involved system which defies analysis, he can usually find a needed document in one of its fifty or more cubbyholes with surprising speed.

Despite his eighty-two years, he continues to display a vigor that has always been an inspiration (and a reproof) to less industrious colleagues. He has seldom absented himself from his post even when troubled with ailments that other men might have regarded as sufficient grounds for indolence — though in later years he has taken a few days off to inspect construction work on a real estate development in which he has an interest. Even if he persisted in this policy, however, he could not expect to regain the time lost in omitted vacations — not to mention night and week-end labor — for at least another two decades.

Fifty-two years ago he began the company; and so any history of the company must begin with him.

That requires a backward glance to 1868. . . .

Part One. The Past

CHAPTER I

The Early Years

1868:

Three years earlier, Grant had conferred with Lee at Appomattox Court House, and the Civil War came to an end.

Millions of young men returned home to resume their shattered lives; but the postwar world was far different from the one that had existed before the appeal to arms.

The industrial cities were now attracting great throngs from the plains; the nation's center of power was shifting from politics to business. Andrew Carnegie, whose gifts would one day be a boon to libraries, was beginning to employ his large fortune in iron to acquire a still larger fortune in steel. John D. Rockefeller, uniting with other tycoons, had created the mammoth Standard Oil Company. Less admirable figures like Jay Gould and Jim Fisk, endowed with the rapacity of pirates, opened a shameful era of plunder. Yet, however dubious their methods, these economic corsairs provided examples of success that inspired a whole generation of Americans. After their incredible triumphs, the Horatio Alger stories seemed merely realistic accounts.

May 12, 1868:

On that day, at Wilmington in the state of Vermont, Halsey William Wilson was born — the son of John and Althea (Dunnell) Wilson.

꙾   ꙾   ꙾

He never really knew his parents, for both of them died of tuberculosis — that dreaded scourge which killed so many in the damp chill of nineteenth-century New England — before he reached the age of three.

Only much later did he learn that his family had a proud ancestry, tracing their lineage back to Roger Williams, the founder of Rhode Island, and to a pair of remarkable women: Anne Hutchinson, the famed colonial heretic, and Mary Dyer, the Quaker martyr who died for her faith on a scaffold on the Boston Common. He discovered even more about his father, a tombstone-cutter, from a folding desk which John Wilson had fashioned with his own hands. The ingenuity of the design, combining beauty with utility, indicated an alert and imaginative mind; and its sturdy appearance was proof of the maker's patience, industry, and skill.

On the death of his father and mother, the three-year-old boy was taken by his maternal grandparents to their home in Shelburne Falls, Massachusetts, and then to a farm on the outskirts of Colrain, in the same state.

It was while preparing for this second move that he received his first book — a copy of the Bible, presented to him as a farewell gift by a neighbor who urged him to consult it regularly as soon as he could read. He gravely promised to do so; and he kept his word. At least, he no longer has the volume, and since he has rarely discarded anything of value in his life, he assumes it must have been worn out with use.

He attended a one-room school near the farm during the winter months. This institution was closed down in the spring and fall because the older children had jobs to perform at home. The remaining pupils were thereupon sent to the schools in Colrain. The transfer meant a mile-and-a-half walk for young Wilson each morning and afternoon; but the long hikes ended when, growing adept at handling a horse, he was allowed to use the family buggy to pick up half a dozen of his fellow students along the way. (He now insists that this entitles him to be regarded as a pioneer in the development of the school bus.)

At the age of twelve, traveling halfway across the continent to live with an uncle on a farm near Waterloo, Iowa, he resumed his education at another rural schoolhouse. He was old enough now to qualify as a "hired hand" and so ceased to be a steady scholar, often abandoning his studies to discharge a multitude of duties about the farm. One of his principal tasks was to guard a herd of twenty cows. This was not an easy assignment, for the shortage of fences in the area permitted cattle, if not carefully watched, to roam for miles about the countryside. Wilson frequently had to remain in the saddle for a whole day at a time, with only his dog, "Shep," as a companion on his lonely vigil.

But he was much more than just a cowboy. He also drove wagons during the harvest season, weeded the vegetable garden, fed the chickens, cleaned out the barns, gathered wood for the kitchen stove, picked fruit in the orchard, delivered messages between the house and the fields, and even found time to sell subscriptions to a boys' magazine as a means of acquiring small prizes.

The problem of recreation never plagued him. Except for an occasional wrestling match during a school recess, he seldom had the leisure for games and sports. If he wearied of a particular chore, however, he always had a simple solution: he undertook a new chore.

He was faithful in his attendance at church services on Sunday, and his aunt supplied further religious instruction during the weekdays. Viewing liquor and tobacco with distaste, she had little difficulty persuading him to adopt a similar attitude toward such temptations; and, having started off on the right course, he "never had much trouble going on" that way in later life.

Three years after his arrival at the Iowa farm, he turned eastward again to become a student at Beloit College in southern Wisconsin. Despite its name, Beloit was a boarding school, not a college. Wilson remained there for two years. Meanwhile, his uncle had retired and, selling his property in Iowa, moved the family to Minneapolis, where his eldest son was studying medicine.

Wilson rejoined them in 1885 and that fall enrolled in the University of Minnesota's preparatory school.

᙭ ᙭ ᙭

The university was then only seventeen years older than the student. It had been chartered by the territorial legislature and granted a large parcel of land by Congress early in 1851. Originally located near the center of the village of St. Anthony, it had been moved to its present site in 1854-55 on a twenty-five-acre plot purchased for six thousand dollars. A single three-story building had been erected and others were planned; but a series of misfortunes, including the financial panic of 1857, forced the school to close.

It was at last rescued in 1867 by the state legislature with a cash endowment of fifteen thousand dollars. The lone building, later known as "Old Main," was repaired and refurnished; a faculty, consisting of a principal and two assistants, was hired; and the school once more resumed its operations.

When Wilson applied for admission, it had become a fairly substantial institution with a student enrollment of three hundred. Two new structures — a mechanic arts building and a greenhouse — had been added to the campus, and other additions were promised. The legislature had voted a six-year annual grant of thirty thousand dollars for new construction — with the warning from one solon that the state would be highly displeased if that sum did not finance all the buildings the school would ever need.

The faculty, though still modest in size, was genuinely distinguished.

It was headed by Cyrus Northrop, a former Yale professor who had been installed as president in the summer of 1885. He impressed one newspaper reporter of the time as "a splendid-looking man, medium height with full chest, broad shoulders, luminous eyes behind scholarly spectacles, polished manners, yet frank and hearty . . ." He loathed keeping records and preferred to discuss problems in face-to-face interviews. Students were encouraged to visit his office, a sunny room on the ground floor of "Old Main"; and many of them — including Wilson — did so. He addressed even more of them at daily chapel, which, despite its noncompulsory character, was always well attended. Northrop was an excellent preacher, skillfully keeping his sermons brief enough to sustain the religious without alienating the skeptical.

William Watts Folwell, who had been the university's first president and still lectured in political science, was equally impressive.

Though he exhibited the courtly manners of a previous generation, Folwell never scorned the ideas of the next, and he often startled the conservative leaders of the community by advocating such radical measures as the five-day work week. Remembering him sixty years later, Wilson recalled a small but imposing figure who somehow retained his dignity even while crossing the campus with a loaded market basket on his arm.

Other faculty members — already at the university or soon to join it — included Willis M. West, an eminent history teacher; George B. Frankforter, chairman of the chemistry department; Frederick Klaeber, a handsome graduate of the University of Berlin who taught Old English; Oscar Firkins, a half-blind critic and dramatist on the English staff; and Lettie M. Crafts, who, under Dr. Folwell's direction, operated the university's modest library.

Probably Wilson's most interesting teacher, however, was Dr. Maria Louise Sanford, the able professor of rhetoric and elocution.

She was a woman of boundless energy who pursued a daily routine that would have killed an ordinary lumberjack. Long before sunrise, she was awake and about her work: chopping wood in the back yard, shoveling snow from the sidewalks, washing clothes for an invalid neighbor, preparing breakfast for the girls who boarded at her house near the campus. Having completed these chores, she bustled off to the university for a seven o'clock class. The regular schedule was from eight to five; but because of the shortage of classroom space, she had prevailed on a number of students to attend a "sunrise" lecture. At noon she usually had lunch, consisting of a large bottle of milk, at her desk to save time. By nightfall, she would doubtless be riding a coach train to a near-by town to deliver an address before some civic organization; and then, bright as ever, she would catch a late train home to Minneapolis.

Dr. Sanford had not been popular with the students during her first years at the university. They felt aggrieved that she demanded so much of them, and her habits of economy made her an obvious target for their ridicule. None of them could know, of course, that she was sacrificing every luxury and many comforts to save as much as possible from her meager salary to repay a debt which, without any dishonor, she might have repudiated. On the advice of a former pupil, she had urged her friends to invest with her in a piece of property that later proved worthless. Rather than dismiss their losses as part of the normal hazards of business, she promised to repay them — and did so after years of self-denial that exasperated her colleagues and students. However, by the time Wilson reached the university, her gifts as a teacher and her qualities as a person were beginning to secure for her an outstanding reputation both on the campus and throughout the Midwest.

⊠   ⊠   ⊠

During his freshman year, Wilson obtained room and board at a private dwelling just off the campus in return for taking care of the owner's horse and buggy. Later he moved to another rooming house and took his meals at a cooperative boarding club called "Bedrock." The girls had a similar club which the ungallant males named "Pullet Ranch." The title of the boys' organization referred to its main regulation: the board rate was not allowed to exceed two dollars a week. The woman in charge of the club's kitchen always succeeded in remaining within the limit set for her, though at times she had to serve bowls of oatmeal for dessert to achieve it. This "bedrock" economy was possible because food sold for prices that a modern housewife would consider fantastic: milk cost only three or four cents a quart, and twenty-five cents bought a bushel of potatoes.

One of Wilson's early roommates was Warren C. Rowell, another student earning his way through school.

The two young men worked together on several jobs, including a morning newspaper route. Since the horse-drawn streetcars did not begin running until six o'clock, they had to leave their rooming house an hour or so before dawn, walk two miles into town to collect the papers, and then cover another five miles to deliver them from door to door. Returning to the Bedrock Club, they devoured a hasty breakfast before rushing off to the campus for an eight o'clock class.

When his partner secured a more comfortable job as janitor of a near-by church, Wilson handled a suburban route alone. The deliveries, made on horseback, took three or four hours. That winter proved one of the coldest in Minnesota's history, with the mercury staying well below zero for an entire month. Wilson was warm, however, in an enormous coonskin coat which almost swept the ground. It had cost him twenty-five of his hard-earned dollars, and he was inordinately proud of it. But any sleepy citizen who glanced out of the window and saw that fur-encased figure riding out of the dawn must have been sorely tempted to crawl back under the quilts.

Rowell was stricken with illness a few months later. Forced to return home to Winona, Minnesota, for a period of convalescence, he induced his roommate to substitute for him at the church and still later, on graduating, arranged for him to inherit the position. Wilson welcomed it because he had now decided to leave the university and study music in the hope of becoming an organist. The new ambition lasted a year. At the end of that time, concluding that music was not his destined career, he once more enrolled at the university.

Yet the year had not been a total loss.

He had been able, first of all, to save a tidy sum by combining his church job with his old paper route. Of course, the combination sometimes resulted in a hectic life. On winter Sundays, for example, he had to start the fire in the church furnace at four o'clock in the morning, pick up his papers downtown at five, return to check on the fire at seven, eat a hurried meal by eight, and then rush back to the church in time to dust the pews and light the gas jets before the service began.

More important, in the long run, than the salary was his friendship with the pastor's son, who had a small press in the basement of his father's home for printing church programs. Wilson was given the chance to buy this equipment shortly after his return to the university. By that time he had acquired a new roommate, Henry S. Morris, the son of a government employee who supervised education on an Indian reservation. Wilson consulted Morris about the offer and since he had no objection to the press as a piece of furniture, it was moved into a corner of their room. The experience gained in its use was immensely valuable to Wilson in later years, though at the time it was treasured solely as an additional source of revenue.

Through the autumn of 1889, the roommates developed an even more ambitious program to supplement their income. The only bookstore in the vicinity was run by a druggist who had reluctantly installed a few shelves in his shop as a convenience to his student customers. Many professors ordered textbooks in bulk from the publishers for their classes; but they, too, resented the extra work. This situation seemed to offer a splendid opportunity. Having managed a bookstore on the Indian reservation, Morris had some training in the business and could obtain credit from the eastern publishers; and Wilson had personal qualities which made him an ideal partner for such an enterprise.

Encouraged by the faculty, the two young men set out to raise the necessary capital. Each in time furnished two hundred dollars — Morris acquiring his share from relatives, Wilson securing his by loans from his fellow students.

On December 4, 1889, the firm of Morris & Wilson was formally launched.

ɴ ɴ ɴ

It began on an exceedingly modest scale, with the partners visiting classrooms, soliciting orders, and delivering the books in person. Nor did they take any chances with failure. During the first year, they continued their paper routes to meet their college expenses and retained every cent of profit from the new concern to promote its expansion.

They were soon conducting such a brisk trade that more spacious quarters became imperative. They had been using their bedroom as headquarters; but now the university came to their aid by making available to them an office in the basement of Old Main. Though far less cramped than a cluttered bedroom, this new abode for their business was still not palatial. Within a twelve-by-sixteen area, the young merchants had to arrange shelves, cases, counters, advertising posters, a cash box, supplies, a mimeograph machine for overnight work on syllabuses — and, of course, provide a few inches of floor space for their patrons.

The building had another disadvantage. When fire destroyed it several years later, Dr. Sanford was not the only spectator who cheered as she thought of "the millions of cockroaches being consumed in the holocaust."

The change in location also created a problem in management. The partners were obliged to schedule their scholastic and commercial activities so as to insure that one or the other would be free to serve their customers. Wilson never really solved the problem: he became so preoccupied with the bookshop that he failed to earn a sufficient number of credits for graduation. Being farther advanced in his academic work, Morris acquired a diploma two years later and departed from the university, leaving his partner in charge of the business. Eventually he sold his share of the company to Wilson when the latter inherited enough cash from his grandfather's estate to permit the purchase.

The store, meanwhile, had flourished.

Then one night Wilson nearly lost everything. He was sleeping at a fraternity house three blocks off the campus when a fire bell awakened him. At that time, on receiving a fire report, the nearest station dispatched a horse-drawn wagon whose clanging bell summoned volunteers to assist the regular fire-fighters. The wagon on this occasion halted in front of Old Main. Pushing through the crowd, Wilson found the blaze centered in the west end of the structure. The store, at the opposite end, seemed relatively safe; but the college library, on the first floor near the middle of the building, appeared to be threatened. Working his way into it, Wilson flung back the escape door leading to the ground and began carrying out the books. He succeeded in removing all of them before the flames reached the library.

As soon as the blaze had been extinguished, the question

arose of what should be done with the books. Wilson finally decided, after noting that the sky promised a clear night, to leave them outside. Since he had no means of communicating this decision to Librarian Crafts, she must have been profoundly startled in the morning to find her books decorating the lawn.

The store continued to thrive, reflecting in its prosperity both the business acumen of its founder and the steady growth of the college community it served.

The original quarters again became inadequate, and an adjoining lecture room was added. The task of supervising the university post office was also assigned to the store, and with this new responsibility, it gained the advantage of daily visits from almost every student and teacher. Nor was the latest fashion, bicycles, ignored. The shop had a large supply of the best models, and the proprietor himself offered to instruct his patrons in the techniques of mastering the intricate machine.

By the beginning of 1895, Wilson regarded his prospects with such confidence that he took a momentous step: he decided to marry. The girl was Justina Leavitt, a student he had met at various social functions on the campus. Now, after a quiet church ceremony in her home town of Sauk Center, they moved into a five-room flat at 227 Eighth Avenue in southeast Minneapolis.

ɴ ɴ ɴ

During the next three years, Wilson built his bookshop into the best in the city.

He was especially proud of the personal service rendered to his customers, advertising that he would "call the attention of those interested in particular lines of study to new books, reviews, and magazine articles in their subjects." This promise was often difficult to redeem. Even locating a specific book was sometimes a considerable feat because of the lack of a convenient trade list of current books. Patrons seeking some new volume might know the author's name, the title, or the publisher; they rarely knew all three facts. The clerk then had to make a tedious search through the catalogs of every publishing house — a disagreeable chore at any time and especially so near the end of the year when the stack of catalogs began to resemble a small mountain.

The harassed bookseller received some assistance from his trade journal, *Publishers' Weekly*, which printed a weekly author-and-title record of new publications and a combined list in a midyear number. That last feature was important, for the weekly records became too numerous after a time. Consequently, when the magazine discontinued the semi-annual list, the bookseller's plight was as desperate as ever.

Surveying the situation, Wilson concluded that he and others of his profession needed a monthly cumulative list; and he resolved to supply it.

CHAPTER II

The Cumulative Book Index

Wilson's decision took him into an ancient field of endeavor.

Since the making of book catalogs was almost as old as the making of books themselves, the first example of such work naturally appeared in Germany, the birthplace of printing. Usually composed in Latin and addressed to scholars, these early efforts were hardly more than advertising hand lists or posters fastened to the walls of churches, universities, student lodgings, taverns, and other time-honored places of rendezvous.

The first comprehensive catalog was issued in 1564 by Georg Willer of Augsburg, the best known bookseller of his day. It was a quarto volume of ten leaves and nineteen pages, recording in a crude classified order more than two hundred and fifty titles published by the leading printers of Germany and Europe. Designed to promote advance sales among those coming to the Frankfurt book fair, Willer's experiment was successful enough to encourage imitations throughout the Continent.

Like their colleagues across the channel, the English printer-booksellers produced their first catalogs for the fairs. But more ambitious ones were soon needed. The hazards of the trade compelled printers to form working partnerships in the production of new books. Each of the contracting parties agreed to furnish a share of the required capital and to dispose of a proportionate number of copies. This cooperative program necessitated a sales catalog for the trade.

The first one was apparently compiled in 1595 by Andrew Maunsell, a former London draper. Presenting a list of divinity books, it was so "well liked of" that Maunsell produced a second list, of scientific volumes, a few years later and was preparing a third, on the humanities, at the time of his death. Book-trade bibliography then languished for twenty-five years; but the service had become so important that others were soon obliged to resume the work.

Half a century after Maunsell's divinity catalog appeared, the first printing press in America was established by Stephen Daye at Cambridge.

The colonial printers, however, did not need a catalog for almost two hundred years. During that period, few books were published in America and fewer still were written by Americans, for knowledge of its domestic origin was always enough to condemn any book in the public mind. As a result, most books were imported from the home country, and so the trade could rely upon English catalogs. The sale of a book, moreover, was then a leisurely transaction; the customer preferred to browse through a shop in search of desirable bargains.

But at last, in 1804, the booksellers of Boston released *A Catalogue of all the Books Printed in the United States* — the first book-trade list in America. This seventy-nine-page pamphlet recorded some thirteen hundred titles, arranged in six major divisions: Law, Physic, Divinity, Bibles, School and Singing Books, and Miscellaneous. Apparently, the movement lacked aggressive leadership; it certainly lacked funds. For one or both of these reasons, the list never reappeared in a new edition.

During the next half-century, the book trade depended largely on the lists that publishers sent out as promotion pieces or inserted in the back of books. The literary journals, particularly the *Folio* of Philadelphia and the *North American Review* of Boston, also helped with literary criticism and comments. Yet none of these were really effective aids. The profession still needed a full-fledged catalog.

Then Orville A. Roorbach came to the rescue of his fellow booksellers.

Born in 1803 at Red Hook Landing on the Hudson River in New York, Roorbach spent his boyhood on his father's farm. He received his education at Albany, became an apprentice bookseller in New York City, and in 1830 moved to Charleston, the wealthiest city in the South, to operate his own store "At the Sign of the Red Bible." Shortly before this transfer, he had begun to gather material for a catalog of domestic books; and in Charleston, between selling chores, he devoted the next twenty years to the project. The first volume of his *Bibliotheca Americana*, a record of twenty-five thousand titles published from 1820 to 1849, was finally issued in the latter year. Roorbach returned to New York City soon after its appearance, and a supplement of two thousand titles was published the following year.

Since the profits from his monumental industry were extremely small, Roorbach had to seek other means of self-support. He held a succession of editorial jobs, opened a new store which quickly failed, printed a trade magazine for some time, and died while traveling as a book salesman.

Charles B. Norton, a purchasing agent for libraries and bookstores, decided in 1851 to continue Roorbach's labors. Early in the spring of that year, he established *Norton's Literary Advertiser*, a monthly journal with book listings, and two years later he issued the first of three annual catalogs. But he soon retired from bibliography to resume his private business. The *Advertiser* was adopted by the New York Book Publishers' Association and continued under various names until it was merged with another magazine to become the present-day *Publishers' Weekly*.

Because of the adverse effect of the Civil War on the book trade, no attempt was made to advance the work of Roorbach and Norton for some time. On the revival of business, however, an Irish immigrant named James Kelly resolved to provide a new catalog. The compiling, done in free moments from his job in a publisher's order department, took three years. Finally, in 1867, the *American Catalogue of Books*, a volume listing some eleven thousand titles issued between 1861 and 1867, was put on the market. The second volume, with an additional seven thousand titles, brought the record down to 1871.

Kelly had hoped to compile a catalog of all books printed in America from its earliest date, but he never acquired sufficient capital for such an ambitious undertaking. It was actually accomplished, at least in part, by Joseph Sabin, whose *Dictionary of Books Related to America from its Discovery to the Present Time* appeared in 1867.

The next period in the development of trade catalogs was vitally important.

Back in 1855 a young German named Frederick Leypoldt had arrived on the American shore. Son of a Stuttgart butcher, he loathed his father's trade, and whenever forced into it, he promptly ran away from home. He was eventually allowed to visit the United States, where, after working in a New York bookstore for two years, he opened his own shop in Philadelphia. It was transferred to New York in 1864, and two years later Leypoldt joined forces with Henry Holt, a recent Yale graduate, to establish a publishing firm. One of the company's publications was an annual *Literary Bulletin*, and in the 1869 number appeared a "Monthly Record of Current Literature," a subject catalog of the principal books issued the previous year. It was followed two years later by the *American Catalogue of Books for 1869*, the first annual catalog since Norton's. A second number was never released, for by 1872 Leypoldt had severed his connection with Holt to publish a trade journal of his own. This journal, combined with a descendant of Norton's original *Advertiser,* became *Publishers' Weekly.*

Soon afterward Leypoldt agreed to compile a catalog of books in print on the guarantee of a certain sum; but in 1875, though only half the necessary fund had been raised, he impatiently began the task. The cost, as usual, far exceeded the estimates, and Leypoldt had to sacrifice his share in the catalog to another company, which published it in 1880. The first two volumes were followed by others at intervals of from five to eight years; and these were supplemented by annual numbers until the series was suspended in 1910.

The booksellers rejoiced, of course, at having these annual numbers. While waiting for one during the year, however, they were compelled to rummage through packs of publishers' catalogs or the weekly records of *Publishers' Weekly.* Responding to their needs, Leypoldt printed a combined midyear list in a July issue; but once more expenses forced a curtailment of the service, and the semiannual record was discontinued in 1895.

That action brought Wilson into the field.

❈   ❈   ❈

Wilson's objective was simple enough. He sought to provide booksellers with a catalog of new books which would remain current throughout the year by combining new entries with old in each monthly number.

This cumulative feature was not new. But it was to be used by Wilson so extensively in the future that it became in time almost exclusively linked with his name. Originally, it appeared to require a vast amount of type resetting for combined numbers and to involve other expenses which even the most opulent publisher could not afford. Out of his experience in printing, however, Wilson devised an ingenious method of escaping many of these difficulties. The lines of type for each entry, he concluded, must be handled like the cards in a library catalog. After their use in a single issue, they could be stored and then combined with new type for the cumulated numbers.

The interfiling of type might seem to be far more complicated than the rearranging of catalog cards; but Wilson flatly disagreed. He was convinced that anyone, with a little practice, could perform the task with speed and efficiency, and he soon proved his point. Members of his staff learned to combine the entries in type at a faster rate than the same entries could have been cumulated on cards.

Wilson spent most of the summer and fall of 1897 planning the new catalog—to be called the *Cumulative Book Index*.

The study entailed a mass of details. What size type, for example, ought to be used? Eight-point was easily read but, in comparison with six-point, would consume twice as much paper and demand more presswork. Consequently, economy being imperative, Wilson chose six-point. This posed a new problem: what should be the length of the printed lines? Not only was six-point type in an extended line difficult to read; the extended line itself caused an excessive number of short runovers, damaging both to the index's appearance and costly in proofreading changes. An overly short line, on the other hand, would create similar perplexities. Obviously, the happy medium was desirable; but the discovery of that medium required weeks of tiresome experimentation. The final decision must have been sound, however, because the type and make-up chosen then have continued to be used in the company's publications for half a century—altered only slightly by improvements in the printing arts.

The style of arranging the entries presented a more intricate problem. After some deliberation, Wilson decided to divide the catalog into two separate alphabets. The first was an author-and-title index. The main author entries included titles in full, number of volumes, size, pages, illustrations, binding, price, date of publication, and publisher. Only a short title and the author's name were to be listed in the title entries. Books were also to be entered in this section under the principal word or catchword of the title. (Thus: "France, the Story of Modern; Lebon, Andre.") The second part of the catalog was to be a classified index — that is, all entries on one subject were to be noted together and all related subjects were to be assembled near each other.

This was a frankly tentative program. Practical experience soon disclosed that the arrangement bewildered the average user. Most of the subscribers favored the alternative dictionary plan. Under this plan, as the name implied, all the entries — author, title, and subject — were collected into a single alphabet. After the first five numbers, the *Cumulative Book Index* became a dictionary catalog.

There was never any question about the location of the new enterprise. The crowded bookstore could not shelter it, and the expense of renting additional space elsewhere would have doomed the catalog before the appearance of its first issue. Only one other alternative remained: the editorial and business office was established in the Wilsons' five-room apartment. The copy was set in type at a downtown print shop, interfiled for cumulated numbers and arranged in page forms at the apartment, and then run off on a commercial press in Minneapolis.

The staff problem was no problem at all. Wilson handled the business details during his hours at home, and his wife agreed to do the editorial work, arranging her household activities to provide the necessary time.

All these economies were essential. With considerable optimism, Wilson had estimated that production costs would amount to five hundred dollars a year. Hoping to attract a great number of booksellers, he deliberately set the subscription rate at a low figure: one dollar per year, ten cents per copy — "for the present." He needed, in other words, five hundred subscribers to meet his basic minimum expenses. While the catalog was gaining this support, the bookstore would absorb the losses; but, of course, it could not continue to do so indefinitely without imperiling its own financial stability.

As the new year of 1898 opened, Mrs. Wilson devoted every spare minute to collecting material for the initial number. She was obliged to rely for information on scattered sources: advertisements, publishers' announcements, literary reviews. The books themselves were seldom available in time, if at all. Nonetheless, near the end of January, the editorial work had been completed. Several hectic days followed while the copy was put into print, inspected for errors, corrected, assembled in forms, and locked on the press. The first number, an unimpressive pamphlet of sixteen pages, was ready in February. The weary publisher delivered the whole edition to the post office by streetcar, and then returned home.

There was nothing further to do now except wait.

⋈   ⋈   ⋈

The first response came from W. W. Waters, who operated a bookstore in Pittsburgh. "It seems too good to be true," he wrote, "that at last we are to have a quick help for the busy bookseller." He wished success to the new enterprise, emphasizing his own faith in the scheme by enclosing a crisp dollar bill. The next day's mail brought subscriptions from John Wanamaker's emporium in New York and from Ellen Plumb, a progressive bookseller of Emporia, Kansas. Before the month ended, twenty-five such letters had been received in the apartment-office of the *Cumulative Book Index*.

No one could describe this as an overwhelming demonstration of support; but Wilson was not at all dismayed. While he sent out promotional material, his wife prepared copy for the second number. She was now so occupied with her dual job of housewife and editor that she cut a little peephole in the windowshade near the door. Thus, when the bell rang, she could discover whether her caller was the grocery boy (welcome) or a social visitor (not at home) without revealing her own presence. Despite such devices, however, the need for a full-time editor became urgent.

The Wilsons found exactly the right person for the position in Marion E. Potter.

Miss Potter was a twenty-nine-year-old graduate student at the university. Printing was no mystic art to her, for she had worked around her father's newspaper shop in Missouri. After attending schools in Freeport, Illinois, she had entered the university to major in languages, principally Old English and Norse under Dr. Klaeber. Though far too retiring to become an outstanding figure on the campus, she must still have impressed her contemporaries since they hailed her in their class annual as "thou living ray of intellectual fire." If more restrained in their language, members of the faculty were equally confident of her ability; and when Wilson sought an editor for the *Cumulative Book Index*, they recommended her highly for the post.

She was terrified by the demands of the job — with some justification. As a graduate student, she had conducted enough independent research to be acquainted with routine library procedures; but she could not be regarded, even with charity, as an expert bibliographer. She had little or no knowledge, for example, of the task of organizing a catalog with proper subject headings. She was not unique in this respect; few people of the period were equipped by training or experience for such work.

But Miss Potter had personal qualities more precious than a specialized education. Even her modesty could not obscure the fact that she possessed an alert and inquiring mind, a conscientious spirit redeemed from gravity by humor, and an extraordinary capacity for work. She was presently so entranced by the job that, according to a favorite company legend, she was startled when presented with her first pay check. "What is this for?" she asked; and when it was explained to her, she exclaimed, "Oh, I didn't know I was getting paid for this!"

𝕩 𝕩 𝕩

Shortly after Miss Potter became its editor, the home of the *Cumulative Book Index* was shifted from the Wilsons' apartment to a small room in the university YMCA building at the gateway to the campus.

There was space in these new quarters, as one veteran employee observed, only for Miss Potter, her stacks of editorial material, and the gasoline fumes that escaped during the process of cleaning ink from galleys of type. A hectic drama often occurred here. As a deadline approached, the downtown printer rushed the type to the *CBI* office; it was combined with the old type; proofs were taken and marked for errors; the galleys were then rushed back to the printer, corrected, arranged into pages, and put on the presses — all at top speed.

Needless to say, under such pressure and with such a system, mistakes were frequent.

One early heading read "Baptists, see also Drunkards." Another identified a member of the British royal family as the "Prince of Whales." Under the title, "Heroes of the American Revolution," in one entry, the publisher's name was supposed to be listed; instead, the following line read "each one sliding off and showing the next." Titles were occasionally misprinted: thus "The Teaming Millions of the East" and "The Church of the Early Bathers." These blunders — amusing in restrospect, nightmarish at the time — were largely the result of working directly with type rather than with copy. Applying himself to this new problem, Wilson designed a multiple process of copy-and-proof checking which eliminated most, if not all, of the errors before presstime.*

* These procedures, as well as other production problems, are discussed in Part Two of this book.

The conscientious Miss Potter sometimes despaired. Certain that she was failing in her duties, she regretted having accepted a position for which she felt ill-trained; but she invariably returned to work after every session of gloomy misgivings with a renewed determination to succeed. She worked through a long day; she worked in the evening; she worked on week ends; and if she ever resented the hours (a highly dubious assumption), she could never reproach her employer for indolence. He was almost as constant in his devotion to the *CBI* as she.

Neither of them could derive much satisfaction from the public support given to the catalog. Only three hundred subscriptions had arrived in the mail by the end of the first year. This was two hundred short of the minimum considered necessary to offset the essential costs. The resulting deficit alarmed everyone — except possibly the publisher himself. Wilson's faith never faltered.

Nonetheless, as his expenses mounted, he was eventually obliged to advance the subscription price from one to three and then to six dollars a year.

The cumulative plan also had to be modified in time. Originally, each issue was complete to the date of publication; but later only three major cumulations were released annually, the intervals between them being covered by single- or two-month supplements. Under the revised schedule, therefore, the initial number of a year reported on books published in the first month; the second combined entries for the two months; a single number was again printed the following month; and a cumulated number, incorporating entries for the first quarter, appeared in the fourth month. The succeeding number was a single-month supplement; the sixth was a double number; and in the seventh month another major cumulation was issued. Then the pattern of supplements was repeated once more through the remaining four months until the year-end annual cumulation. Under this program, the user of the index never had to consult more than three catalogs at any time to keep informed of the current books.

Any saving that might have resulted from these changes, however, was more than canceled by the expenses of a new bibliographic venture.

×   ×   ×

The *Cumulative Book Index*, an up-to-date record of current publications, only partially filled the booksellers' needs. They also required a combined trade list of books in print in the United States. Wilson sought to provide this additional tool in the autumn of 1899 with the first edition of his *United States Catalog*. The title reflected his interest in simplified spelling — an interest which had a practical basis. He estimated that it meant a five or ten per cent reduction in printing costs. But it also had its disadvantages. One librarian, declining to subscribe, explained his decision by stating, "Anyone who does not know how to spell catalogue won't make a good cataloguer."

The initial number of the *Catalog* was arranged in two parts: an author index compiled by Miss Potter and a title index compiled independently by George F. Danforth, librarian of Bloomington, Indiana. Later editions (four in number, the last of the series being published in 1928) were organized into a single author-title-subject alphabet by the Wilson company staff.

The work of creating such a volume appeared simple enough, at least from a distance. All Miss Potter needed to do was obtain a price list from each publisher, compose several entries for every book, collect them into one alphabet, and print, bind, and distribute them to a waiting public.

But this simple chore could become infinitely complicated.

It began, as an employee once wrote, with a letter to every publisher: "We ask for *three* (3) copies of his latest complete catalog. In reply comes a most courteous letter.

He is delighted to comply with our request — and sends one copy. We write again with the gentle patience that we regard as the chief of our virtues, and perhaps eventually obtain our three copies." But the complete catalogs were not always complete; and sometimes they were overcomplete, containing out-of-print books and even books of other publishers. One catalog listed a book in six different places, and in only two entries was there agreement as to the author's name, the title, and the price.

The publishers, moreover, were seldom in haste to inform the Wilson company of price changes, though on occasion it received a series of letters like this: "July 7: List the book at $1.25." "July 8: Since writing you yesterday . . . list it at seventy-five cents." "July 8: Since writing you this morning . . . So kindly change it to $1 and oblige." Yet this publisher was more highly cherished than those who simply ignored every inquiry.

The persistent editors also had their moments of triumph. "How in the name of the devil," an amazed author once wrote, "did you folks get hold of my full name? I've kept it a dead secret."

The writers of privately printed volumes were always cooperative, often sending a pathetic note along with their books. "Although that is the price I mentioned," one of them declared, "I would not have you understand that it could not be bought for less. I fixed that price simply because I do not think that, as an author, I ought to undervalue my own work." Another writer, obviously confused about the purpose of the Wilson catalogs, complained that he had waited in vain for a reply after sending a copy of his latest book. "If it is no good in your estimation," he added mournfully, "then please throw it in the Mississippi River."

Nor was the staff, in its concentration on the details of compiling, ever allowed to forget that the books were woven out of human happiness and suffering. One author wrote to announce that his work had been delayed by neuralgia, a severe cold in several vital organs (all of them enumerated), and an attack of rheumatism in both legs. Another reported gallantly: "The revision of the book . . . has not been complete owing to an unfortunate train of mishaps, including fire, Pasteur treatment on account of the bite of a rabid cat, blood poison, three surgical operations, and a number of minor misfortunes — not helped by a depression and several printers' strikes. . . . I am sorry to send out a book not entirely revised, but the loss of five months' time, about $20,000 in cash, and a square foot of skin interfered with my previous plans." After such messages, the staff felt guilty in subjecting the volumes to the hard-and-fast rules of cataloging.

The 1899 *United States Catalog* was followed by three completely revised editions in 1902, 1912, and 1928. The last was a huge twenty-seven-pound tome as compared with the seven-and-a-half-pound volume in 1899. The comparison reflected the change in American publishing during the years — and also the principal reason why no further editions of the *Catalog* have come from the Wilson presses. With the enormous increase in published titles and the reduced life-in-print of the average book, an "in-print" catalog became not only fantastically expensive to produce but of constantly decreasing usefulness. It was believed, therefore, that the permanent five-and-six-year volumes of the *Cumulative Book Index* (which in 1929 had become a "world list of books in English") would be of greater value. Though more alphabets must be searched for the complete record, it *is* the complete record — not just a list of titles that happen to be in print at an arbitrary date.

❈   ❈   ❈

Determined to produce a model catalog, Wilson made frequent improvements in his publications. Early in the spring of 1899, for example, the whole *Cumulative Book Index* was thoroughly revised and in large part rewritten so that the entry for each book might contain the full name of the author, the exact title as found on the title page, and other useful data that had been previously omitted. Similarly, the first edition of the *United States Catalog* had hardly left the presses before plans were inaugurated for the vastly expanded second edition.

These changes, of course, necessitated an enlarged staff; and as the editorial force grew, the need for more space became pressing. Accordingly, the office was transferred to the top floor of a building in the university neighborhood, and then in 1900 to a new two-story structure just off the campus. The bookstore and the publishing office were installed on the main floor; the basement was sublet to a printing shop (later purchased by Wilson); and the second floor was rented to college dancing parties.

The expansion increased the gap between the company's income and expenses.

As a means of promoting his publications, Wilson obtained the services of his old classmate, Warren G. Rowell, who had been a credit supervisor in a Minneapolis department store and a book salesman since his graduation from the university. Wilson induced him to carry the catalogs as a side line on his selling tours; and when the experiment succeeded, Rowell was hired to work for the company on a full-time basis.

Despite his missionary work, however, the deficits continued to mount. Wilson was now devoting almost all the profits from his bookstore to the publishing concern — with seemingly little hope of recovering his money in a reasonable length of time, if at all. Indeed, he occasionally feared that he might not be able to pay his hard-working editors, and once or twice he actually had to ask them to wait a few days for their salaries.

Nonetheless, despite this constant anxiety, he refused to be discouraged. On the contrary, instead of abandoning his costly projects, he was already planning still another one.

CHAPTER III

The Readers' Guide

Although conceived as a short-title catalog for book-sellers, the *Cumulative Book Index* gradually acquired a number of library subscribers who found it useful as a guide in their purchase of books and in preparing their own card catalogs.

For that reason, as well as to seek professional counsel in bibliography, Wilson began to attend local and state library conferences, where he heard many laments about the difficulties of locating specific articles in the mass of current magazines. Delegates from the smaller institutions, in fact, often questioned the wisdom of retaining back issues of periodicals in the absence of a prompt indexing service.

Actually, at least three periodical indexes existed at the time; but all of them were considered unsatisfactory.

The first in seniority had been started by William Frederick Poole. While a junior at Yale and librarian of one of the student literary societies, Poole had noticed that the library's sets of standard periodicals, though rich in research material, were seldom consulted. As a result, he compiled an index to some of these magazines which proved so popular that the manuscript was soon tattered with use. Since the only way to preserve the work was to publish it, he issued a 154-page booklet in 1848 under the title, *Index to Subjects Treated in the Reviews and Other Periodicals*. The five hundred copies were quickly sold, and Poole set out at once to produce a larger volume. The new edition, with six times as much material, appeared in 1853 and, like its predecessor, was rapidly exhausted.

Almost three decades elapsed before another revision emerged. Meanwhile, Poole had held a succession of important library posts that prevented him from continuing the work. Though he diligently sought for someone to take his place, he was unable to find an acceptable candidate; and, with the growth of the magazine industry, the task became impossible for a single person to perform.

At the first meeting of the American Library Association in 1876, therefore, Poole proposed that the next edition be compiled as a cooperative enterprise. Under his plan, various libraries throughout the country (some fifty eventually participated) would be assigned certain sets of periodicals. The cataloging would be done, without charge, on small cards after regular library hours; then the cards would be sent to a central office to be consolidated into one alphabet and prepared for the press. The project received the endorsement of the association, and Poole was named editor-in-chief.

After a series of delays, the index finally appeared in 1882 — to be supplemented during the next quarter of a century by five-year volumes.

Unquestionably, Poole's catalog was a notable achievement, and it still remains a unique record. Yet, with all its virtues, it was also highly defective. It was difficult to use because it cited a magazine's volume number rather than the date; it was extremely limited in scope; and some of its indexed periodicals had little or no reference value. But perhaps its most grievous fault was its infrequent publication. During the five-year intervals between supplements, librarians were left to struggle unaided with the flood tide

of magazines. Some tried to maintain a current catalog of
their own. This desperate effort was expensive in time and
money; and, since the work was being duplicated in a number of places, it was also wasteful.

The problem was temporarily solved by the *Cooperative
Index to Periodicals*, which first appeared in the spring of
1883. Edited by W. I. Fletcher, one of Poole's early colleagues, it was supplied with material by members of the
American Library Association and issued as a monthly supplement to the *Library Journal* until the end of 1884. At
that time, under financial pressure, it became a quarterly;
but even this program was apparently too ambitious, for in
1889 it was changed to an annual.

In abandoning its monthly and then its quarterly schedule, Fletcher's index lost its timeliness and thus much of its
merit. At the American Library Association conference in
1895, therefore, the delegates listened attentively while
William H. Brett of the Cleveland Public Library proposed
a third attempt to furnish a prompt service.

For a number of years, Brett reported, his staff had been
compiling for its own use a card index to reference periodicals. It was now ready, on the basis of that experience, to
edit and publish a monthly catalog if encouraged to do so.
Receiving the convention's blessing, it proceeded to issue
the first number in 1896. Each number, under the original
plan, was to be fully cumulated, but production costs and
inadequate support once more compelled some modifica-
tions. Only quarterly cumulations were printed after 1899; a
private concern absorbed the project in the same year; and
the whole enterprise soon appeared doomed.

By that time (1901) Wilson had launched his *Readers'
Guide to Periodical Literature*.

※   ※   ※

While planning this addition to his list of publications, he
had been careful to re-examine the history of its predeces-

sors. One conclusion at once seemed inescapable: bibliographic work was so expensive in comparison with its returns
that it could not succeed on a purely commercial basis.

The early editors of periodical indexes, in recognition of
that fact, had sought editorial aid from their colleagues.
Poole had even attempted to make a virtue of the necessity.
"When we begin to pay for service," he once wrote, "the
knights leave the line, and their places are filled with retainers and camp followers." Actually, Poole could not afford
the retainers and camp followers even when, as sometimes
happened, the knights sulked in their tents. For the librarians, though willing to donate time and labor, were reluctant
to contribute cash.

This sort of editorial cooperation was really futile because
it began at the wrong end — at the producer rather than the
consumer end. The dependence upon volunteer catalogers
separated from each other by vast distances caused endless
delays that reduced or destroyed the essential value of an
index. Obviously, the editorial work could be done efficiently only in a central bureau, with the costs shared by the
subscribers. The Cleveland project, however, appeared to
cast some doubt upon the feasibility of this solution.

But did it?

The Cleveland Public Library had charged a flat rate for
its service. Owing to heavy expenses, the price was too high
for the financial capacity of most small libraries, but too low
to produce an adequate income. Thus the dilemma: a further reduction in the rate would be instantly disastrous; yet
without a reduction the subscribers would remain limited
in number.

How could this dilemma be escaped?

The librarian of Johns Hopkins University had a suggestion: convicts should be set to indexing under competent
supervision. "The kind of labor proposed," he asserted, "is
peculiarly suited to the reformatory idea, being incompara-
ble for teaching order, patience, humility, and for thorough-

ly eradicating the last trace of the Old Adam in whoever pursues it." Poole, considering this prankish letter to be a slur upon his work, wrote a highly indignant reply.

More seriously, a device used by some of the specialized indexes seemed to offer hope: the entries were printed on separate cards to enable a librarian to purchase just the sets he needed. With a bound catalog, of course, he had no choice in the matter: he had to pay for the entire index regardless of whether or not he found all of it useful.

Intrigued by the card scheme, Wilson did some figuring on the comparative costs of printing cards and a book. The answer was sixteen to one in favor of the book—a result easily remembered because William Jennings Bryan, running for President that year, had insisted that a sixteen-to-one ratio of value ought to be established for gold and silver.

The outcome of the cost comparison might have startled anyone who had no knowledge of printing. But Wilson knew (and his calculations proved the point) that editorial and typesetting costs up to the press-run of an index remained the same whether the work was performed for one or one thousand subscribers. Moreover, the cost of multiplying copies was comparatively small. The cards, on the other hand, would be much more expensive for libraries to handle. They would have to purchase storage cabinets, assign floor space, hire expert filers; and in time, of course, the card catalog would become inconvenient in size.

The scheme was reluctantly shelved. The price of the *Readers' Guide* was set at the standard flat rate, and it promptly started losing money.

As the debts mounted, Wilson experimented with a scale of prices based on the subscriber's ability to pay. Libraries were divided into classes according to their incomes, and each class was charged a different fee. But this system rested on the questionable assumption that the index's value to a subscriber could be measured in terms of his wealth. It seemed much more reasonable to vary the charges in proportion to the actual *use* made of the *Readers' Guide.* Certainly, the library with only five of the periodicals covered by the index did not receive as much service as the library with ten. Charging them both the same price was as unjust as establishing a flat sum for both large and small consumers of electricity. The card scheme was based on this principle of use; and if the scheme itself appeared to be impractical, that fact still did not discredit the principle.

Thus was born the "service basis" plan under which subscribing librarians were expected to pay for the *Readers' Guide* in proportion to the number of the indexed periodicals they took. Proving generally acceptable, the policy was applied in modified forms to other Wilson company publications and was responsible in a large measure for rescuing the firm from its financial plight.[*]

❊   ❊   ❊

Being a product of a central staff of catalogers, the *Readers' Guide* was not marred by one of the major flaws of the earlier indexes. Poole and his associates, in organizing their entries, had used the original titles of the articles instead of grouping them under a common subject heading of their own selection. The dangers inherent in such a method were clearly recognized in their instructions to the cooperating indexers. "The references," the fifth rule read, "will be made as brief and comprehensive as possible. In most instances the author's own title best expresses the subject of his paper; but if the author has given his article an obscure or fanciful title, the indexer will give it a better one and place it under the heading where it naturally belongs. . . ."

Conforming to the policy of using titles whenever possible, the indexers listed similar articles under "Mausoleums," "Burying Grounds," "Cemeteries," or "Graveyards." This lack

[*] Since the "service basis" is a highly complex subject, it is discussed fully in a separate section in Part Two of this book.

of uniformity did not trouble the editors. "Could it not be said in all fairness," one of them asked, "that the choice of different names for their treatises by different writers warranted the inference that the subjects were diverse?" Moreover, as another pointed out, any attempt to connect similar articles would transform the index into a book of cross-references. The practice was further defended on the grounds that anyone using the index would be sufficiently astute to know that he must pursue his subject through several related classifications. "The alphabetical arrangement," Poole declared, "is so simple that the stupidest mortal can understand it without explanation."

The assertion was swiftly disputed.

Referring to Poole's astute user, a librarian submitted a set of inquiries: "Does he know 'without explanation' that he must look under the North Pole, Polar Sea, Beechy, and other headings if he wants to get at the literature of Arctic exploration? Or that he must look under general heads if he does not find what he wants under the special head? Or that if he does not meet with success in England, he must look under the adjectives English and British — to say nothing of Great Britain? Or that he will find a subject entered at one time under its country, another time under its subject, and sometimes under both or, worse still, under neither?"

Other examples might have been cited. If the reader wished to locate material on labor unions, he was obliged to look under Labor, Associations of; Labor, Organized; Labor associations; Labor organizations; Labor Unions; Trade-unionism; and Trade-unions — with no cross-references to guide him from one to the other. Because of the use of both singular and plural forms, Jew was separated from Jews by five other classifications. Articles on alcoholism were scattered under Alcoholism, Alcoholic excesses, the Drink Question, Drunkards, Drunkenness, Inebriates, Inebriety, Intemperance, Liquor, and Temperance. Even the wisest mortal might be forgiven if he could not bring all these headings readily to mind.

Most of Poole's critics agreed that his reliance upon titles in compiling his entries was a fundamental error that reflected a false premise. It was true that a book catalog had to include title entries, for the general public rarely remembered books in any other way. Magazine articles, on the other hand, were ordinarily recalled by subject and not by title. If this assumption was true (and experience seemed to justify it), then the compiling of the two types of indexes ought to proceed on different plans. The book catalog should contain both title and subject entries, with emphasis on the titles; the periodical index should concentrate on subject entries, with titles added as finances permitted.

But Poole really had little choice in the selection of his cataloging system under a cooperative program. It would have been virtually impossible for fifty collaborators in widely separated areas to agree upon proper subject headings — much less upon the assignment of articles to them. Such work could only be the product of a well-integrated staff laboring under the supervision of a single editor-in-chief.

※　※　※

That situation existed at the Wilson company.

Aided by a corps of assistants, Miss Potter assembled material for the *Readers' Guide* when free of her duties on the *Cumulative Book Index* and the *United States Catalog.* (Precisely how she accomplished all this will remain a mystery forever.) But because she did most of the work herself and constantly checked the work of others, the old system of title entries could be discarded for the alternative system of author-and-subject entries, with a liberal use of cross-references. *

Even this plan, of course, had some disadvantages. It

---

* The methods of compiling the *Readers' Guide* and other Wilson indexes are described in detail in Part Two of this book.

would be difficult — one might just as well say impossible — to develop a faultless plan. The use of inverted subject headings, for example, was necessary to reduce the number of entries under one heading without dispersing them throughout the index. Thus: Education, Compulsory; Education, Higher; and Education, Secondary. This could be inconvenient if the researcher looked first under Compulsory Education, Higher Education, or Secondary Education; but it would not be much more than inconvenient. For cross-references would lead him to the inverted headings; and despite the momentary delay, the value of finding all articles on one subject in the same place was still worthwhile.

The first number of the *Readers' Guide,* issued originally on a monthly and years later on a semimonthly schedule, indexed twenty periodicals. As more and more magazines were included, the work became burdensome even for the indefatigable Miss Potter, and another editor was sought to take her place. At the University of Minnesota Library, Wilson found Anna L. Guthrie, a graduate of the New York Public Library School. She assumed editorial charge of the *Readers' Guide* in 1903.

That same year the rival *Cumulative Index to Periodicals* of Cleveland was absorbed, bringing John B. Doster, its publisher, to the Wilson company as business manager.

[*Mr. Lawler's statement, above, that the first number of the* Readers' Guide *indexed twenty periodicals, was based on the best information available when he wrote it. However, subsequent investigation, at the time of the* Readers' Guide *fiftieth anniversary in 1951, disclosed that the true first issue—published as a "supplement" to the* Cumulative Book Index—*included only seven periodicals. For a detailed account of the founding and early history of the* Guide, *the reader is referred to the* Wilson Library Bulletin, *April 1951.*—PUBLISHER]

CHAPTER IV

The Minneapolis Years

The company had now arrived at a point in its development when a complete reorganization became necessary.

Accordingly, in the spring of 1903 it was incorporated, and shares of preferred stock (valued at a hundred dollars each) were sold to employees, librarians, faculty members of the university, and other old friends of the enterprise.

Two years later, having already outgrown its rented quarters, the firm needed additional capital for the construction of a larger building.

The proposed site was a vacant lot directly opposite the main gateway to the campus on the corner of University and Fourteenth avenues. Wilson had purchased this property at an earlier date for three thousand dollars, one third in cash and the rest on a mortgage. Someone had promptly offered him twice that amount for it; but disregarding expert counsel, he had declined to sell. The lot, as he told one of his advisers, was worth much more than that to him; and he proceeded to demonstrate it.

First of all, he formed the "South East Minneapolis Building Company." The H. W. Wilson Company, in return for ten thousand dollars' worth of its common stock, transferred the lot to the new concern. Then ten thousand dollars' worth of its preferred stock was sold to the public—two thousand dollars being used to pay off the mortgage and the rest being applied to the construction of a modern fireproof structure. A fifteen-thousand-dollar loan was also obtained from a local bank, the lot serving as collateral. The "South East Minneapolis Building Company" then agreed to lease its building to the H. W. Wilson Company for a term of twenty-five years at a rental sufficient to pay the five per cent interest on the loan, an annual six-hundred-dollar reduction on the loan, and a seven per cent dividend on the preferred stock. Thus, with a thousand-dollar cash investment, Wilson acquired a property worth at least thirty-five thousand dollars.

The transaction received an unusual accolade. It so impressed a bank president in Minneapolis that he discussed it at length before a state banking convention. "As you look at the building," he told his colleagues, "you might say to me: 'That building is of brick and stone.' But I tell you that building is a creation of the mind. You might say to me: 'That building is built by capital.' But I say to you that building is built by courage. As we look at that splendid structure, we forget the men and teams who made the excavation; we forget the masons who laid the brick and stone; we even forget the architect who drew the plans. We remember and admire the young man who saw that building as a vision in his mind before fingers were touched to pencil or hand was laid to shovel."

Originally the company occupied only two of the building's three stories.

The basement housed the recently acquired print shop, and the main floor was divided between the bookstore and the indexes. The store, in the front of the building on Fourteenth Avenue, took most of the space. The editorial staff, numbering about a dozen people, was crowded into a small back corner on the east side of the building. On the opposite side was a miniature business office, completely filled by the desks and files of Business Manager Doster and his assistants.

The top floor was at first rented for fifteen dollars a night to college parties and meetings; but it was eventually taken over by the company. The editors' relief at their escape from the crowded quarters of the first floor was accompanied by a feeling of intimidation; they were overwhelmed by the surrounding areas of emptiness. The reaction was only temporary. As more people joined the firm, the old sense of being imprisoned in a small cell returned.

*   *   *

Wilson sometimes feared, in view of all this expansion, that his company might be losing its family character.

The staff bulletins, issued at irregular intervals, always stressed the theme that everyone must unite in a common effort to promote the highest interests of a unique organization. It might not be possible for each employee "to get a sweeping perspective of what the institution as a whole" was designed to accomplish; but he was solemnly assured that his "little part well done" should be considered essential.

But Wilson was not satisfied with exhortation. He sought to determine exactly how every employee regarded his work. "Is it with enthusiasm," he asked in an interoffice memorandum, "that you begin the daily task or is it with a sense of heaviness and inertia? What is the matter?" If working conditions did not encourage harmony, he wanted to know about it. "Let each one," he proposed, "consider his relation to his job and see me during the month of May, bringing with him plans, suggestions, and troubles. Office hours for this purpose will be from 1 to 2 p.m. daily."

The fact that every member of the staff could have a private interview with him in a month of one-hour sessions ought to have reassured him that the company had not yet become an impersonal colossus.

Most of the clerical workers were graduates of a near-by high school. They came to the company with the blessing of their parents, who rejoiced to have them employed in an office far from the business center of that wicked metropolis across the river. The Wilson building, however, was not a gloomy institution. On the contrary, it was often a gay place — particularly at noon, when many of the young ladies, having brought their own lunches, spent the half-hour break in a circle around Miss Potter's desk.

Miss Potter, of course, was an inspiration. As in most firms of the period, the girls had to work nine hours a day and six days a week. The schedule might have been a cause of dissatisfaction, but it was embarrassing to complain when Miss Potter set such an exalted example of industry. Nothing seemed to daunt her. One evening a snowstorm lashed the city, blocking traffic with enormous drifts and preventing a majority of the staff from reaching the office the next morning. Miss Potter was among the absentees at first, but, several hours late, she bustled into the building; she had walked from her home through four or five miles of snow. At about the same time, the newspapers reported that a heroic dog in Alaska had performed a similar feat in rescuing some storm-trapped miners. Most readers were impressed with the saga, but not the Wilson employees. They knew Miss Potter.

Hers was not merely the joyous courage of youth. Almost half a century later, Miss Potter became involved in a losing argument with the wind one day and was slapped to the ground, breaking a leg in her fall. Transported to a hospital, she telephoned the office a few hours later to insist that a stack of magazines be brought to her for indexing. After all, she had nothing to do, she said, except wait for her broken leg to mend.

There were, naturally, other factors that contributed to the high morale of the office force.

Women formed the bulk of the staff. Ordinarily, they

were welcome only in teaching and related fields, but Wilson offered them an opportunity to advance in a rapidly expanding enterprise. Thus their jobs, though rarely dramatic, opened a pathway to an exciting future and promoted a sense of high adventure.

Moreover, the company was always cordial to new ideas. Everyone was encouraged to suggest changes in procedure that seemed desirable in the light of his own on-the-job experience. The policy paid dividends: many of the firm's basic techniques resulted from staff proposals. Wilson himself stimulated initiative by his own inventiveness. He was constantly revealing new discoveries to his startled associates. It might be a clever device for quickly computing overdue fines on a library book; or an improved "chase" for locking type for the press; or a portable truck for transporting volumes around the stacks of a library; or an ingenious method for ensuring editorial accuracy; or simply another bibliographic service to his customers. Some of these ideas never survived the discussion stage; others failed in practice. But Wilson was never depressed by the failures or complacent over the successes. He just produced another idea; and his persistence inspired others to be equally resourceful.

Yet, undeniably, the most important element in morale was the company's size.

It was possible to speak of the firm, with almost literal accuracy, as a contented family. Nor could anyone hoot derisively when he read these words in the employee journal: "Just as in a large family the entire number is exalted by the high achievements of its brilliant members and brought low by the failures of its less successful ones, so here in our workshop the fine efforts that call forth laudation bring honor to all of us and incompetence and failure leave stinging disappointment in their wake." These remarks had an obvious motive: they were intended to promote efficiency. Nonetheless, they would never have been written if the nature of the company had not seemed to warrant them.

If the family atmosphere was ever an illusion, Miss Potter must be charged with being one of the chief magicians. She endeared herself to her staff by inviting them to dinner at fashionable restaurants during the Christmas holidays and by taking them to plays at the old Opera House in the theatrical season.

The Wilsons, too, were noted for their hospitality. Even in the lean years, they held a Yuletide party for the office in their home. These festive affairs invariably ended with "Three cheers for Mr. and Mrs. Wilson!" — given, as a veteran employee now confesses, "partly because of the good time we had enjoyed and partly because of the gifts each of us carried home." There was also an annual summer picnic — with a romantic moonlit boat ride which was responsible, no doubt, for a number of intra-office marriages.

Other acts of kindness were performed in secret. On one occasion, the husband of a staff member misappropriated some funds at the bank where he worked as a clerk. When the matter was brought to his attention, Wilson not only settled the boy's account, but arranged for him to start anew in the company's printing department.

Though the staff could rely on such paternalism, they were, nonetheless, seldom allowed to forget their own obligations.

Thus a notice on the office wall: "The company furnishes individual towels to each employee and expects that each shall hold himself responsible for his own towel. In case of loss, he shall pay the cost of the towel, which is eight cents."

The sober attitude of some workers was also instrumental in maintaining self-discipline. One J. W. Tracy, for example, writing for the Wilson house organ, deplored the swift tempo of living. "We are drifting along," he lamented, "without compass or rudder to guide us. We look for 'a good time' rather than its consequences. We should wake up to the strenuous necessities of a more useful and active life." As an alarm clock, Tracy urged the formation of a company debating society. "It would be a good plan," he wrote, "if we familiarized ourselves with the 'pros and cons' of such subjects as Canadian Reciprocity, Parcel Post, and the Municipal Dance Hall. These questions are all vitally interesting and well worth anyone's careful study."

It may be questioned whether anyone on the staff ever became an expert on Canadian Reciprocity, Parcel Post, or the Municipal Dance Hall. On the other hand, no one could have been a mental laggard while men like Tracy were present to apply the righteous rod. That may even have been part of the place's charm. At any rate, old employees recall this pioneering period with a strong mixture of pride and pleasure.

*   *   *

Early in the winter of 1905, the H. W. Wilson Company dispatched to its subscribers an eight-page prospectus for a new magazine to be known as the *Book Review Digest*.

"For many years," the announcement read, "the question of the evaluation of literature has been much mooted in library circles." Then as evidence it cited the opinions of more than a dozen librarians. Such proof was hardly necessary. Practically everyone in the field admitted that a library, regardless of income, could not afford to buy every book; that the choice of the best involved an exercise of judgment; and that the judgment of even the most learned must depend upon outside advice to some degree. But unanimity ended there. When discussion advanced from the problem to the solution, librarians disagreed. Some advocated descriptive appraisals and others preferred critical estimates; some wanted an expert's verdict and others spoke of "the collated result of the views of several men"; some insisted on separate lists for each branch of learning and others demanded a single survey of all new books. Eventually, after protracted debate, they did agree that the desired service ought to furnish (1) brief descriptive statements for each book and (2) the opinions of several responsible critics.

On the best means of organizing such a service, however, they were once more divided. Most of the suggestions envisioned a whole new machinery of evaluation staffed by pundits in every division of the arts. The scope of these plans discouraged even their authors.

Wilson's program for the *Book Review Digest* was much more modest.

He proposed to condense the best critical work appearing in some forty independent publications. (An additional forty were added in time on the basis of votes cast by a representative group of subscribers.) More than half these sources were to be authoritative organs like the *Political Science Quarterly*; about a fourth were to be general public magazines and newspapers; and the rest were to be scholastic or library journals. No book was to be noted unless reviewed by at least two of these selected periodicals.

The *Digest* was to be printed monthly, with quarterly cumulations. (Later only semiannual and annual cumulations were supplied, and the monthly number in July was dropped. A subject-and-title index was cumulated in every issue, however, and a five-year index appeared in every fifth annual.) The magazine was to be divided into three main sections. The first was a list of the regularly surveyed periodicals. The second contained the main entries in alphabetical order under the author's name and included pertinent facts about each book (price, paging, publishers, etc.), a descriptive note, and excerpts from the reviews. The cumulated subject-and-title index formed the third section.

Clara E. Fanning, a member of Mrs. Wilson's sorority at the university, was brought into the office to edit the new publication. Receiving part-time aid from Mrs. Wilson in the early years and later commanding the services of full-time assistants, she developed an intricate system for compiling material, a system still used by the present-day editors.

As the required two copies of the periodicals arrive in the mail, they are sent to a filing table where each review in them is carefully marked. The title of the book is outlined in brackets; the author's name is underlined; and the article is stamped with the name of the magazine, the date, and the volume and page numbers. The reviews are then cut, folded so that the title remains visible, and roughly filed alphabetically under the author's name in a row of cardboard boxes. At a later date they are more precisely arranged in another file and the reviews pertaining to each book are assembled and clipped together.

Two editorial precautions are taken at this point.

The last annual number of the *Digest* and the current number are examined to determine whether the reviewed book has already been noticed. If it has appeared, the new reviews are set aside to be inserted in a future cumulation.

The second check involves a standing or "repository" file. This collection contains reviews of those books which have been judged by only one of the listed periodicals. If no further criticism is printed of them, the single reviews are discarded at the end of the year; but if another review does arrive, the two articles are brought together for processing.

For each reviewed book, a member of the staff prepares a small card, inscribing the title and author at the top left-hand corner and indicating with a symbol whether the book itself has been received from the publisher. This card, filed alphabetically by author, is inserted in a drawer marked for the issue in which the book is scheduled to be entered, thus forming a record of the books in each number of the *Digest*.

A second card (in reality, a heavy manila folder) is also prepared. The author's name and the book's title are once more written in the upper left-hand corner. On this folder are pasted the reviews for that particular book, with the number of words in each clipping noted directly below it. After a study of these reviews, one of the library-trained editors encloses in brackets the lines to be extracted for quotation. The excerpts, selected to offer a faithful statement in brief of the critics' judgment, usually run about a hundred and fifty words or less. They carry plus or minus signs to indicate whether their general trend is favorable or adverse. Occasionally, a combination of symbols is necessary: a plus followed by a minus for favorable with some reservations or a minus with a plus for unfavorable with incidental praise. Not all the reviews are so rated, however. Some of them are quoted merely as useful statements of fact when the attitude of the critics cannot be determined.

Then a descriptive note is written for each book.

Based on an examination of the book itself or on other relevant material, these notes have to be concise and non-evaluative. The difficulties of this apparently simple chore were once well suggested in a letter of instruction composed by a former *Digest* editor: "Avoid expression of personal opinion. But, if you can, express something of the spirit of the book. Transmit the author's point of view. This can sometimes be done in his own words. . . . Keep the note well under two hundred words. Remember that our notes will be scanned hastily. Librarians haven't the time to read long expositions. . . . Give the table of contents when not too long and when chapter titles are informative. . . . Give information about the author when his position has a bearing on the subject. . . ." The letter of counsel continues for three pages and concludes: "Avoid scrappiness in notes, i.e., quoting from several sources. Seek for unity of impression. . . ."

The final editorial task involves the choice of subject headings to be cited in the main entries and again in the subject-and-title indexes. The *Digest* staff generally accepts the headings assigned by the *Cumulative Book Index* or by the Library of Congress, but it selects its own on occasion.

Accompanied by the descriptive notes, the folder-cards are then turned over to a typist, who from them prepares the copy for the printer on long sheets of paper.

The *Book Review Digest* was an almost instantaneous success — though a rare dissent has been heard. Once its editors were severely scolded by an author for quoting only adverse criticism of his novel. "If you maintain that item to be (in line with the title of your magazine) a digest of the reviews," he stormed, "I take pleasure in telling you that you lie. And the intention behind the preparation of such an item is — I choose the word with the greatest care — contemptible."

That accusation of black-hearted villainy has ever since been cherished by the editors as an antidote for gloom.

☙ ☙ ☙

Shortly after the company moved into its new quarters near the campus gateway, the university librarian appeared one afternoon with an urgent appeal. He had recently discovered to his horror that one of the volumes in a treasured set of the *Review of Reviews* was marred by a section of wear-soiled pages. The rest of the volume remained in its original pristine condition. This puzzle was easily solved: students in a public speaking course had been consulting an article in those pages for a class debate on capital punishment. Resolving to prevent any further ravaging of his valuable sets, the librarian learned in advance the topic for the next debate, collected a number of pertinent articles, and came to Wilson with a request to have them reprinted.

This was not the company's first service in the field of debate literature. For some time it had been publishing a pamphlet for the Minnesota High School Debating League, an organization supervised by the university's extension division. The booklet, distributed to member schools, contained information about the league and a selection of magazine articles on questions recommended for debate. Moreover, as publishers of the *Readers' Guide*, the company had received a steady stream of letters inquiring about copies of certain indexed articles. Recognizing another opportunity for service, Wilson had established the Cumulative Reference Library department to assemble such material for loan or sale at a small fee. It had been welcomed by clubwomen, politicians, industrial leaders, writers, and others; but by far its best customers were debating societies in the rural Middle and Far West whose local libraries were inadequate. Eventually, when university and state library extension services began furnishing reference material, Wilson closed his own department; but at the moment it was a thriving part of the firm.

These experiences led to the *Debaters' Handbook* series.

The first title, on the enlargement of the United States Navy, was compiled in 1907 by Miss Fanning. After that number, however, Edith M. Phelps assumed editorial charge of the series.

Miss Phelps was another of the remarkable young women who helped to build the company. She had taught school in southern Minnesota at a time when the life of a rural teacher demanded Spartan virtues — particularly in the winter, when ink wells had to be buried in the stove ashes over the week end to prevent them from freezing. Nor was her salary munificent: she received twenty-eight dollars a month. Yet, out of that meager wage, she was able to save enough to pay her tuition and board at a state normal school. After completing her courses there, she taught again for two years and then enrolled at the university to specialize in mathematics and philosophy. She worked as a proofreader at the Wilson company while a student on the campus; and on obtaining her degree (and a Phi Beta Kappa key), she was hired to handle promotion. Now in 1907 she also became editor of the new publication project.

She chose topics for the series only after studying the list of debate questions selected each year by college and state high school leagues. The titles, therefore, mirrored the swiftly changing issues of the day. One of the early pamphlets was concerned with the proposed income tax; another with the initiative and referendum; still another with woman suffrage. (The latter must have exerted some influence upon its editor, for soon after its release she became the treasurer of the Minneapolis suffrage organization.) Despite the controversial topics in the series, the company was only once accused of promoting a subject for its own political purposes. A pamphlet on the "Metric System," though apparently innocuous, brought forth an indignant letter charging the publisher with working "hand in glove" with the Communists.

It was a point of honor with Wilson that the series editor should read, or at least examine, every relevant article during the preparation of a handbook. When the subject was new, this duty was easily performed; in some instances, indeed, the problem was really to locate sufficient material. But more often Miss Phelps had to comb through a haystack of words in pursuit of a few worthwhile needles. Probably her most difficult assignment was the League of Nations handbook. Published at the height of the argument over American participation, it went speedily through edition after edition and had to be revised constantly in the light of new material. At the end of a frenzied year, Miss Phelps was grateful when interest in the subject declined.

As more schools engaged in debate, a corresponding growth occurred in the literature devoted to it. Various local, state, and regional debate leagues began issuing booklets which discussed, usually in terms of personal experience, the art and rules of debating. Wilson decided that the best of these articles ought to be collected into a single volume, and the result was the *Debaters' Manual*. The idea must have been sound, for the book had to be returned to the presses for six printings to satisfy the demand. Still later the company launched its *University Debaters' Annual* series, a compilation of each year's outstanding intercollegiate debates.

The *Debaters' Handbook* series evolved in time into the *Reference Shelf*.

The little books in this new series, though still useful for debaters, are designed to be background volumes on general problems — immigration, racial prejudice, world peace, inflation — rather than collections of pro-and-con arguments about a specific measure. They provide a broad picture of a contemporary issue, including statements on its development, the proposals advanced in regard to it, and the reasonable comments made for and against those proposals. Sold by subscription (six titles a year) or on a single-copy basis, the books consist of extracts from authoritative speeches and leading journals. Though prepared for the press by the Wilson company editors, the material is now for the most part selected by outside experts. The editors cut the articles judiciously, since otherwise the same data and arguments would be repeated over and over again in only slightly different form; and they preface each section with a brief introduction to unify the book and aid the reader. Bibliographies are added to encourage further study.

Under the direction of Miss Phelps, who acted as editor of general publications until her retirement in 1947 after forty years of service, the company has also published a considerable number of other books — most of them tools for librarians and speech instructors. One of the best known of these has been *The Library Key*, a practical guide to the use of libraries, which has sold extensively through six editions. From the Wilson presses, moreover, have come such items as yearbooks of holidays, a dictionary of World War II slang, collections of library plays, reading lists on various subjects, anthologies of jokes, color-illustrated books of wild flowers, an index to reproductions of American paintings, a compendium of slogans, a life of Carrie Chapman Catt, and several biographical series. Most successful in the last-named have been the collective biographies of musicians and composers by David Ewen and the author books — *American Authors, British Authors, The Junior Book of Authors*, and *Twentieth Century Authors* — edited by Stanley J. Kunitz and Howard Haycraft. There have also been bibliographies on such subjects as juvenile delinquency, radio and television, American history, dancing, motion pictures, the Virgin Islands, swimming, vocations, Cervantes, the Negro, and cooperative farming — to mention only a few.* Many of the early books were written by Minnesota faculty members, and so the company functioned as an unofficial publishing unit for the university.

With the exceptions noted, the Wilson books have rarely been money-making ventures, and some of the bibliographies have been such heavy losers that the company seldom publishes any of them today without a guarantee from an outside organization.

Though Wilson objects to an over-all deficit on the book-publishing operation, he does not expect it to register a profit. He seeks to supply useful volumes; and, by doing so, he hopes to create good will within the library profession as well as contribute to the company's prestige. It is difficult, of course, to gauge his success in this respect; but from Africa one day came a request from the King of Uganda for a copy of the *Bibliography of the Negro in Africa and America*. True, the monarch was so dilatory about paying for the book that the business manager had to write him a tart little note, which began, matter-of-factly, "Dear King." However, the order at least proved that the company's reputation was world-wide.

× × ×

During the autumn of 1911, Wilson negotiated an agreement which further strengthened his company's position.

---

* A chronological list of the company's miscellaneous publications will be found in Appendix II.

He and R. R. Bowker, owner of *Publishers' Weekly* since Frederick Leypoldt's death, had been engaged in a polite form of warfare for more than a decade. The *Cumulative Book Index,* as recorded in these pages, had been started when *Publishers' Weekly* dropped its semiannual list of current books. The *CBI* had been on the market only a few months, however, when the trade journal re-entered the field by printing quarterly and annual cumulations. Four years after the birth of the *Readers' Guide,* moreover, Bowker had issued another monthly periodical index. On the other hand, Wilson published a digest of library literature that competed with the *Library Journal,* and his *United States Catalog* of books in print duplicated in some measure the *American Catalogue.* Both the *Journal* and the *Catalogue* were published by Bowker.

Necessity compelled a truce. The vast expansion in book and magazine production had made indexing so expensive that neither man could afford to continue the useless struggle. They agreed, therefore, to coordinate their activities.

Under the new arrangement, Bowker discontinued the quarterly and annual cumulated lists in *Publishers' Weekly,* suspended publication of his *American Catalogue,* and dropped his periodical index. Wilson, in turn, promised to provide more thorough coverage in the *Cumulative Book Index,* added to the *Readers' Guide* the magazines that had previously been indexed only by its rival, transferred to Bowker his directories of booksellers and librarians, and allowed his digest of library literature to be incorporated in the *Library Journal.* (Twenty-five years later, after Bowker had dropped the feature, Wilson started *Library Literature,* another index of books, pamphlets, and magazines related to the library profession.)

The compact was mutually profitable, but it was also a recognition of the Wilson company's success — a success achieved far from the eastern center of publishing.

The founder derived some satisfaction from that isolation. But he realized that he paid for his midwestern site in inconveniences that seriously hampered his business. Time was lost as books and periodicals, the company's raw materials, traveled nearly halfway across the continent to Minneapolis; and further delays occurred as the indexes journeyed eastward again to reach the Atlantic seaboard, where many of the firm's major subscribers were located. Warren G. Rowell, who had recently opened a branch office in New York City, helped to expedite the distribution of the company's products; but the growing volume of sales was more than he could handle at a distance from the home office. Furthermore, his presence in the East did not solve the vexing problem of tardy mail service.

By the early summer of 1913, Wilson had concluded that he could no longer sacrifice the timeliness of his publications by remaining in Minnesota. The whole enterprise must be transported to New York. With great reluctance, he disposed of his bookstore to a competitor. The shop had supported the indexes out of its profits for sixteen years, but now the indexes exceeded it in importance. By midsummer, the moving began. This was a monumental undertaking. Files had to be assembled and locked; the company's library had to be boxed; presses had to be dismantled; type had to be cleaned and packed; office furniture had to be hauled to the station — and all this had to be accomplished without interrupting the publication schedules. But at last the caravan of fourteen fully loaded freight cars pulled out of the Minneapolis railroad yards.

It was almost more difficult to persuade key members of the staff to make the eastern journey. Only about twenty agreed to move — enough, however, to form a nucleus around which a new staff could be organized. Wilson shared their sadness at leaving; and, hoping to lessen the blow, he supplied each of them with sufficient cash (in addition to their transportation) for stopovers in Chicago and Niagara Falls.

The new headquarters were in White Plains, some twenty-five miles north of New York City, in a large single-floor garage which had been transformed into an office building by the erection of glass partitions.

Married employees soon found homes in the vicinity. The single girls scattered to various rooming houses, but most of them boarded at "Mother Tomkins'" where steaming clams — strange fare for inlanders — awaited them at almost every luncheon. Loneliness persisted for a time, of course. The staff felt stranded in White Plains, then too small in itself to provide diversions and too distant from New York to permit frequent trips. Wilson did his best to console them by arranging for the use of a local swimming pool and bowling alleys, and on hot summer days he took many of them out to the near-by beaches in his car.

But perhaps the best remedy was work, and the editors had a full measure of that cure. For, as usual, the company was launching several new publications.

Expansion in the East

The next three decades were a period of astounding growth as the usefulness of the *Readers' Guide* created an incessant demand for more specialized indexes.

The *International Index to Periodicals*, the first of almost a round dozen new indexes, was begun in 1907.* Originally released as a supplement to the *Guide* and later as an independent publication, it was an author-and-subject index in dictionary form to magazines devoted to the humanities and pure science: history, economics, psychology, philosophy, political science, international relations, and some twenty other subject fields. It served a different audience from that of the *Guide*. Public libraries were the latter's best customers. The new index found its principal subscribers in college, reference, and special libraries. The "special" category included those maintained by divinity schools, business firms, study groups, government agencies, and even motion picture studios, which presumably used the publication in locating background material for historical films.

In 1913 the company issued the first number of the *Indus-*

* Details — coverage, content, schedules, etc. — of these and other indexes will be found in an alphabetical list of the company's serial publications and services in Appendix I.

trial Arts Index, a guide to the increasing number of technical magazines. Its title was somewhat misleading. Though covering science, engineering, and industrial journals, it also indexed periodicals in such fields as economics, advertising, banking, insurance, printing, and public administration. Miss Potter edited the new publication for several years in addition to her duties on the *CBI*; but eventually even she could not continue to perform such a miracle of industry. Another editor was hired for the *CBI*, and Miss Potter retained editorial control of the *Industrial Arts Index*. Fearing that she had been "too slow" in handling both jobs, she was saddened by the change; but she was soon so engrossed in the new work that she did not have time for further regret.

Wilson became the publisher of the *Index to Legal Periodicals* and the *Public Affairs Information Service* in the following years. The first of these, compiled by members of the American Association of Law Libraries, still remains with the company. The information service, a cooperative venture of legislative libraries and others interested in providing a catalog to public affairs literature, later became an independent organ, though it is still printed by the Wilson press.

The *Agricultural Index* first appeared in 1916. Like the *Industrial Arts*, it was far broader in scope than its title implied. It covered not only general agricultural journals, but periodicals in related fields like botany, bacteriology, conservation, entomology, forestry, and home economics.

For more than a decade thereafter the company was too occupied with other matters to consider extending its list of periodical indexes. The existing publications demanded constant care to make them at least self-sustaining; World War I posed grave new problems in management and personnel; other forms of cataloging seemed more urgently needed; and, above all, the search for a new location consumed a great deal of time, money, and energy. The suburban site in

White Plains, which had appeared so eminently desirable in 1913, was regarded with discontent four years later. This was partly due to its limited size, partly to its remoteness from New York, and partly to the owner's reluctance to institute any basic improvements in the rented property.

Consequently, after surveying every available spot in New York City, Wilson purchased a five-story brick building on the east bank of the Harlem River, in the Highbridge section of the Bronx, at a bargain price of thirty-eight thousand dollars.

Miss Phelps directed the transfer in the fall of 1917. With an intricate floor chart indicating the position of each piece of equipment, she settled one department at a time into the new structure. Thus the interruption in the regular work schedule was kept at a minimum. Space was so abundant at first that the company even contemplated leasing one of the floors to an outside concern; but, as of old, the crowded condition soon reappeared. The congestion was relieved by the erection in 1929 of an eight-story building to the south of the original quarters and in 1938 by another six-story addition to the north. Even these proved in time to be inadequate, and in 1946 two adjoining garages were acquired for storage purposes.

The move from White Plains naturally involved changes in personnel, and the recruitment of new staff members was particularly difficult in a period of wartime labor shortages. Because of these dislocations, Wilson's plans for other periodical indexes had to be postponed. But in 1929, just before the economic storm broke over the nation, he turned his attention back to that field of endeavor.

The result through the years was an impressive calendar of achievements:

1929:

The *Education Index.* This guide to educational literature had been proposed by some prominent teachers as early as 1905. At the time, however, the company's facilities had been so taxed by earlier commitments that the request could only be answered with a promise that such an index would be started as soon as possible. By the fall of 1928, the firm was at last in a position to redeem its pledge, and the initial number of the index appeared in the spring of the following year.

The *Art Index.* Covering art magazines and museum publications, this proved to be one of the company's most expensive undertakings.

1932:

The *Vertical File Service Catalog.* A subject index-catalog that records current, available pamphlets and similar material, with descriptive notes and prices.

1935:

The *Abridged Readers' Guide.* As more and more magazines were indexed by the *Readers' Guide,* librarians in smaller institutions began clamoring for a supplement embracing only a limited number of periodicals. This new index answered their requests. In form it was exactly like the larger publication, but it indexed only about thirty magazines.

1936:

The *Motion Picture Review Digest.* Learning that libraries were clipping movie reviews for use in advising parents about the best films for children, Wilson started the *Digest.* It was abandoned four years later when other organizations began issuing recommended lists and the movie industry itself submitted to voluntary censorship.

Library Literature. An index to books, pamphlets, and periodicals related to the library profession.

1938:

The *Bibliographic Index.* A subject index to bibliographies, both those published separately and those published as parts of books, pamphlets, and magazine articles.

1940:

Current Biography. A monthly magazine supplying up-to-date biographical sketches of people in the news.

1946:

The *Biography Index.* A one-place subject index to biographical material in books, pamphlets, and periodicals, including an index by professions and occupations.

※ ※ ※

As already noted, the development of new periodical indexes had been delayed in part by Wilson's desire to undertake other forms of cataloging which seemed more urgently needed.

Some of this cataloging was designed to solve the problem of library book-selection — a problem with which Wilson had been concerned almost from the beginning of his work in bibliographic publishing. He was aware, as were all librarians, that the public library stood for a certain dignity in the choice of books. Tradition alone demanded that volumes on its shelves should be, not the most expensive or most popular, but the most useful books on the market. Its patrons had come to look upon it as a source of dependable books. It was expected, in other words, to set a standard.

But what were the best books?

Certain qualities were obviously desirable. The books, first of all, had to be recognized by experts as valuable. They had to be scholarly works of undisputed standing in their fields; they had to be complete, well written, ably edited, clearly arranged. But they also had to be measured in terms of their usefulness. Every authoritative book, of course, could not survive this test; some of them were too technical in nature, too restricted in appeal, and too narrow in scope. Though adding prestige to the library that owned them, these volumes would be suitable only for a large reference institution. Economy, too, was an important factor.

Though endorsed by specialists, a book might be available only in an expensive edition. Thus it might not be a wise purchase for a library with limited funds — and all libraries had more or less limited funds.

How was a librarian to know the best books?

Wilson's *Book Review Digest* offered some help; but it covered only current publications and depended for its selections upon two or more reviewers whose competence could not always be known. Various "best book" nominations were also useful. It was fashionable at the time for almost everyone — teachers, authors, printers, ministers, poets — to compile his own particular list; but, naturally, each list mirrored only the compiler's individual preferences. The situation really demanded a catalog of books whose soundness had been approved by acknowledged experts and whose usefulness had been confirmed by experienced librarians.

The company's first experiment in this field of selective bibliography was its *Children's Catalog* of 1909. As the title indicated, this was a list of books (fiction and nonfiction) of interest to children. It has been kept up-to-date ever since by the publication of five-year revisions and annual supplements.

Nine years later the first section (on sociology) of the *Standard Catalog for Public Libraries* appeared. Other sections on philosophy, literature, biography, history, fine arts, and so on were later published and then arranged into a single list.

This catalog, covering only nonfiction books, now includes a basic volume listing some twelve thousand books, with annual supplements, cumulated frequently, each containing six to eight hundred titles. After several years, the supplements and the basic volume are revised and combined with new material to make a new basic volume. The catalog has several uses in addition to the obvious one of guiding book purchases. Because of its classification and index features, it can be consulted as a reference tool in locating books on a specific subject, in seeking material on a particular topic, and in preparing library catalog cards.

The catalog is divided into two parts, plus a directory of publishers.

The first part, arranged under the Dewey Decimal Classification system, offers a complete listing of each book — including author, title, copyright date, publisher, retail price, subject headings, and a brief description of the book prepared either by the Wilson staff after a study of the book itself or extracted from a review in a recognized source. Single paragraphs of critical evaluation are also frequently cited, and books related in subject matter to the main entry may be noted as supplementary reading. Books recommended for first purchase by small libraries are marked with a star; those especially recommended receive a double star.

The second section of the catalog consists of a straight dictionary index by author, title, and subject and by analytical entries referring to parts of the listed books.

(This arrangement, and the procedures about to be described, vary only slightly on the other catalogs in the series.)

The cataloged books are tentatively chosen on the basis of reports in twenty-three prepublication lists and library bulletins. If these sources suggest that a book has considerable merit, an "authority card" is made for it. Several months before their deadline, the catalog editors re-examine the cards and compile a preliminary list, arranged in classified order, for submission to a group of "collaborators."

The collaborators (between fifteen and fifty for each catalog) are staff members of representative libraries throughout the United States and Canada, aided by recognized specialists in judging technical volumes. They mark the lists with special symbols for six gradations of votes: outright rejection, a questioning without positive disapproval, approval, recommendation for first purchase by small libraries or by very small libraries, and an admission of unfamiliarity with the book. They are requested, in addition, to propose other titles for separate entry or supplementary reference.

Meanwhile, back in the Wilson office, record slips have been pasted to the bottom of the authority cards. When the preliminary lists have been returned, the votes for each book are transferred to these records, and a numerical evaluation that takes into account both positive and negative votes is made of them. The results are noted on the cards. This whole operation, from the sending of the lists through the tabulation of the votes, ordinarily requires about a month.

The selected books are then studied by the editor assigned to annotate the authority cards. These annotations, as previously stated, often include two paragraphs: a general description of the book's contents and an evaluative note derived from some reviewing medium. Finally, the classifications chosen for the books at the time of compiling the tentative lists are inspected again and changed if it seems desirable. On the basis of the authority cards, the books themselves, and other material, a typist then prepares the copy for processing.

The *Standard Catalog for Public Libraries* and the *Children's Catalog* were the forerunners of many similar publications.

They include: the *Standard Catalog for High School Libraries,* a basic volume of forty-five hundred fiction and nonfiction titles with semiannual supplements; the *Fiction Catalog,* an index of works of fiction in the English language consisting of a basic volume (revised every ten years) and annual supplements; the *Essay and General Literature Index,* which analyzes books of essays in all fields and other important reference works of a composite nature; the *Educational Film Guide,* a monthly classified list of 16 mm. nontheatrical films, with quarterly cumulations (including a selected list) and an annual volume; the closely related *Filmstrip Guide*; the *Song Index*; the *Short Story Index*; and the

Readers' Choice of Best Books, a monthly listing of fifty-five books which appears as the second section of the *Wilson Library Bulletin,* but which can also be purchased separately for library distribution.*

The company also began a printed catalog card service in 1938. Books to be cataloged are selected on the basis of reports from various libraries, critical reviews, preview mediums, library bulletins, and prepublication material. Cards are automatically made for all major book club selections.

Two different sets of cards are available — the number in a set varying with the complexity of the book but averaging four or five. One set ("with") carries the Dewey Decimal Classification numbers and subject headings at the top; the second ("without") lacks this printed information at the top because some librarians prefer their own style of markings. Libraries can purchase all the sets on an annual subscription basis or individual sets for eight cents each (sixteen cents for the first set in each order). A coupon system is used to reduce bookkeeping costs.

New titles, about thirty-five, are added every week. The fact that a book has been included in the service is noted in the appropriate standard catalog and in the *Cumulative Book Index.* A supply of cards for each book is maintained as long as it remains in a catalog.

￼ ￼ ￼

Though the periodical indexes are valuable guides in the often arduous pursuit of information, they are, naturally, useless without the periodicals themselves.

It might delight the soul of a researcher, for example, to know that he could find a significantly titled article in an issue of the *Arya,* a philosophical review published in Pondicherry, India; but where — except possibly in Pondicherry — could he find that issue of that magazine?

* Further information on these and other catalogs may be found in Appendix I.

The likelihood of his receiving an answer to such an inquiry was exceedingly remote until 1927, when the Wilson company published the *Union List of Serials*, a massive volume listing more than a hundred thousand serial holdings in institutions throughout the United States.

The *Union List*, doubtless the greatest cooperative enterprise ever undertaken by American libraries, began on the local level when libraries in metropolitan districts started compiling records of their own periodical holdings. Some of these had been printed by Wilson. Then P. L. Windsor, librarian of the University of Illinois, proposed a regional list. "As you know," he wrote to Wilson in January of 1912, "I am interested in securing the publication of a Union List of Serials in the larger libraries of the Middle West. . . . If Michigan and Wisconsin and one or two others could also furnish 'copy,' don't you think some arrangement might be made for issuing within a couple of years a Union List?"

Wilson promptly agreed. "We shall be very glad indeed," he assured Windsor, "to cooperate with you in your effort to stimulate interest in this plan." There ensued five years of discussion to settle countless questions on matters of policy and style.

Should some limit be established for the number of volumes listed for incomplete sets of serials?

Should every periodical holding in every cooperating library be listed?

Should all the midwestern libraries be invited to participate or just those which had originally indicated some zeal for the project?

Should the cost of the publication to each library be determined by the number of entries furnished by it? Or should the cost be divided by the size of the edition and each library be required to take a certain number of copies at that price?

Should a provisional edition be issued?

Should the libraries be identified in the entries with abbreviations? If so, what system should be adopted to ensure uniformity?

Should valuable government serials be included?

Should definite information in regard to title changes be placed only in the main entry or should it also be . . .

The catechism need not be continued. The questions stated are typical of scores of others upon which the co-operating libraries and the company had to agree before the work of compiling the list could begin in earnest. But, finally, in the summer of 1917, all the points at issue had been reconciled and the project was begun.

The contract for the book opened with these words: "The undersigned libraries of the North Central States do hereby agree to engage the H. W. Wilson Company to publish for them a union list of periodicals in the libraries of the North Central States, in accordance with the specifications listed below . . ." One of these specifications stated that the cost, covering manufacturing charges and the editorial work performed by the company, was not to exceed $5.20 per page for an edition of one thousand copies. As a result of the post-war inflation, however, this proved to be a wildly optimistic estimate. Less than three years after negotiating the contract, Wilson found that the per-page cost had advanced to seven dollars. The libraries, meanwhile, had encountered obstacles of their own in compiling the entries.

Near the end of 1921 the project appeared doomed unless, as some librarians advocated, it could obtain greater support by being broadened into a national list.

Wilson decided upon an experiment to test the feasibility of such a scheme. He had his staff prepare a leaflet listing some seventy-five periodicals extracted from earlier union lists. This was sent to fifty of the nation's largest libraries with the request that they mark their holdings among the magazines cited in the pamphlet. Thirty-one institutions did so. On the basis of their replies, Wilson then printed and distributed sample pages to illustrate the plan, scope, and value of the list. The resulting discussion aided him in devising a program for its compilation and financing.

The method of compiling was to be similar to the one employed in the experiment. First of all, a list of thirty thousand or more titles would be organized by using the existing local union lists. This would be sent to the larger libraries of the country in printed form with sufficient space between titles to permit each library to indicate its holdings. Upon the return of the checked list, a complete record would be made and printed in a provisional edition. Since many libraries, through exchanges of partial sets, were expected to make major changes in their holdings, a revised edition would be published a year or two later.

Wilson thought the publishing of the checking, provisional, and permanent lists would require three years of work and thirty-six thousand dollars. "It has been suggested," he wrote, "that there are thirty-six large libraries in the country which would be willing to underwrite this undertaking to the extent of one thousand dollars each payable in annual or semi-annual installments." If thus protected against loss, the company was prepared to conduct the enterprise without profit.

At the midwinter meeting of the American Library Association in Chicago, Wilson outlined his proposal and asked that an advisory committee be appointed to cooperate with the company in its execution. His request was granted. The committee, headed by Harry M. Lydenberg of the New York Public Library (and, in Lydenberg's absence, by Princeton's James T. Gerould), was largely responsible for promoting the necessary guarantees. Some forty or more of the larger libraries agreed to purchase twenty-four copies of the *Union List of Serials* at fifty dollars a copy. This arrangement produced a fund of about fifty thousand dollars. For his part, Wilson invested several thousand dollars in the preliminary editorial work and renewed his pledge to publish the list on a nonprofit basis. He also offered to open his books at any time for inspection by the advisory committee; but the members never took advantage of this offer — an implied tribute to Wilson's integrity. However, the company did render periodic statements on finances and progress to the American Library Association.

The schedule of publication followed closely Wilson's original outline. The checking lists were distributed soon after enough guarantors had been obtained; the provisional edition appeared in 1924; and three years later the permanent volumes were delivered to the subscribing libraries. By the middle of 1930, sales had been sufficient to create a surplus of nearly ten thousand dollars. The guarantors were then asked whether this sum should be paid back to them in cash or in the form of a supplementary volume. They chose the latter method, and the supplement was issued in the summer of 1931.

The *Union List of Serials* was an acknowledged success.

Five years later, in the spring of 1936, Wilson began questioning librarians about a new edition. During the planning of the original work, it had been assumed that many changes in periodical holdings would result from the publication of the list. Actually, fewer transfers and consolidations occurred than would seem desirable; but there were other factors that stimulated interest in a revision. The first edition had not covered adequately all sections of the country, and a number of special and smaller libraries, which had been ignored in the first list, now wanted to be represented. After a year's survey of the situation, Wilson returned to the American Library Association with a request for another advisory committee.

Two meetings with this committee, under the chairmanship of James T. Gerould, were held in New York. The first was primarily concerned with such matters of detail as the inclusion of more libraries, the addition of certain types of periodicals, the use of symbols to indicate institutions having photostat facilities, and the possibility of condensing the records of holdings by various typographical devices. At the second conference the prospect of obtaining a grant to finance the editorial work was discussed at some length, and Wilson agreed to furnish tentative estimates on the cost. Gerould resigned his post as chairman shortly after this meeting. He was replaced by Donald B. Gilchrist, librarian of the University of Rochester.

That change produced one of the rare instances of discord between the company and librarians.

Though Wilson had previously been invited to attend all committee meetings, he was not informed by Gilchrist of the latter's successful efforts to obtain a forty-eight-thousand-dollar grant from the Rockefeller Foundation. Then — again without Wilson's knowledge — the committee appointed an editor, fixed her salary, and opened offices in the Library of Congress for work on the new edition.

When these facts came to his attention, Wilson addressed a letter to Gilchrist and his fellow committeemen. "As we see it," he wrote, "the present relationship between the Advisory Committee and this Company should be and is identical with the relationship during the time when the subvention was secured from larger libraries for the previous edition. It does not seem to us that a change in the source of the subvention should transfer the ownership of the publication itself from the Wilson Company to the Committee. . . . We wish to have it definitely understood by all concerned that the *Union List of Serials* is a publication of the Wilson Company, that the management of the editorial work, printing, and publishing is to be carried on by the Wilson Company with the cooperation of the Advisory Committee. . . . We should go back to the methods and plans that worked so successfully for the first edition."

Gilchrist replied that if the *Union List* belonged to anyone, it belonged to the American libraries. "Certainly," he declared, "without the full cooperation of the libraries, no publisher could make a decent list; and certainly not without the fund-raising powers of the Advisory Committee could either the first or the second edition have been financed." He was convinced that the editorial work could be accomplished more efficiently and economically at the Library of Congress than at the Wilson plant. Unless evidence to the contrary could be presented, he saw "no reason why the Committee should bow to a claim of authority over the *Union List* on the part of the H. W. Wilson Company."

Nothing can be gained at this late date from a detailed account of the controversy that raged over these conflicting viewpoints. Yet the dispute did occur and, for the sake of historical accuracy, cannot be ignored. It revealed, moreover, that a venture in bibliographic publishing could be imperiled by such intangibles as natural misunderstandings and personality clashes. But eventually the quarrel was settled with a compromise. The committee assumed the role of author, being responsible for the preparation of copy; and the company exercised the rights and privileges commonly conceded to a publisher (except that the right to a profit was waived). Questions regarding the scope of the list, the size of the edition, and other elements of mutual interest were decided in joint conference; and the greatly expanded Second Edition appeared in 1943. Thus the *Union List of Serials* remained the greatest cooperative enterprise ever undertaken by American libraries — and perhaps the initial difficulties only emphasize the magnitude of the achievement.

� ✾ ✾

The Wilson indexes converted periodicals into such valuable sources of reference material that Ralph Munn once counseled his fellow librarians in case of fire to "save the magazines — let the books burn." This was sound advice. Most of the books could be duplicated or replaced by other editions; the magazines were often priceless possessions. Ordinarily they had a brief life, traveling from press to rubbish heap in a matter of days; by the end of a single year many of them had become great rarities. Yet they also formed the core of a library's reference section. The loss of them, therefore, would immeasurably weaken any library.

The new importance of old magazines naturally led to a steady demand for them.

Aware of the need, Wilson established in 1910 the Periodicals Clearing House, a separate branch of the firm assigned the task of buying, storing, and selling back-number copies.

This department has since grown into the largest business of its kind in the world. Its present stock, occupying almost thirty thousand square feet of floor space in the Wilson buildings, consists of about three million odd-number copies, a hundred thousand volumes of bound copies, and a thousand complete sets. It can furnish copies of popular magazines like the *Atlantic* or technical journals like *Comptes Rendus des Seances de l'Academie d'Agriculture de France.* It is particularly vigilant in maintaining a supply of important scientific, scholarly, and professional reviews appearing in the standard indexes. No effort is made, however, to stock such items as detective stories, movie magazines, or the "pulps."

Most of the periodicals are purchased from libraries. Institutions within a radius of a hundred miles of New York send their unwanted magazines by freight in gunny sacks supplied without charge by the company. They promptly receive cash or credit memorandums for the shipment at prices which compare favorably with those paid by other concerns. Libraries at a distance consult a "want list" published at regular intervals. (The latest edition listed about eighteen hundred different titles.) There are also truck pickups at city libraries, private homes, and industrial firms. The publishers of some magazines like *Time* contribute their overrun copies, and occasionally a visit to a local magazine shop may produce a long-sought number.

Three record cards are kept for each periodical title: one for single copies, the other for odd volumes, and the third for complete sets. These files provide a full and continuous account of all stock on hand, with information concerning the shelf locations. Some idea of the complexity of this record-keeping can be gained by remembering that every issue of about six thousand different periodicals constitutes a separate item for which a special entry must be made.

For the sake of convenience, quick-moving magazines are kept on the first of several floors used by the department for storage purposes. This arrangement has to be flexible, for next year's fast-selling items may differ radically from this year's. The demand for periodicals faithfully reflects the latest trends in research and so changes swiftly. At times, too, some special issue of a magazine will become suddenly popular. During the prohibition era, for example, a scientific journal carried a technical article on the making of Scotch whisky. When this was cited in a Wilson index, the requests for copies of that issue deluged the office.

Orders range in size from single numbers at the minimum charge of sixty cents to huge consignments costing as much as twenty thousand dollars. (The selling price of any magazine is only slightly controlled by the available supply and demand. The expenses of bookkeeping, storage, interest on long-range investment, and other overhead are much more important factors.) More than eighty-five per cent of the ordered periodicals can be shipped directly from stock. They are brought down to a collator's table, and every page of every issue is carefully inspected for defects. Only rarely does an imperfect copy escape detection; and when such a mishap does occur, the company promptly sends a replacement. The order is then weighed to determine the most economical method of shipment and forwarded.

The whole process usually requires anywhere from one to thirty days. However, if the customer insists upon a complete set, the difficulty of locating one may sometimes delay the order for months or even years.

Domestic libraries, of course, are the best patrons of the

service, but institutions in almost every land have occasionally sent orders. Probably the best foreign customers at the present time are Russia, Holland, Italy, and the Scandinavian countries. (England would be on that list if currency restrictions did hamper her purchases.)

Viewed from the outside, the operation appears impressive in size but certainly not fascinating.

The staff would probably disagree with the latter part of that statement. They have the satisfaction of performing a much-needed task and sometimes feel the excitement of a sleuth in tracking down an obscure journal. With considerable justification, they can also cherish the thought that a periodical shipped by them may inspire a vital scientific discovery or a practical plan to ensure world peace. Moreover, speaking of peace, they may even be able to detect a meaningful trend in the nature and source of some orders. During the years just before the Pearl Harbor attack, the Japanese secured from the company a vast collection of American technical journals. Today the Russians are ordering similar publications in equal volume. But before the reader hastens to a storm cellar, he should be reassured with the fact that the Soviet Union has always been a steady customer for such material. History, in any case, seldom repeats itself in quite the same way.

꙰ ꙰ ꙰

This survey of the company's past would not be complete without a brief mention of two of its periodical publications which do not fall into the index or catalog patterns.

The *Wilson Library Bulletin* is one of these. Begun in 1914 as a company house organ, it has since been transformed into a professional subscription magazine (monthly except in July and August) which publishes articles of service and interest to the whole library community, with a strong accent on practicality. In addition to its general articles, it includes regular monthly departments devoted to school and children's libraries, extension services, special libraries, the American Library Association, current reference books, biographies of new authors, a literary calendar, library publicity, and the like. It also publishes several topical numbers each year on such subjects as Book Week, public relations, and vacation reading. The magazine has a wide popular appeal, its paid subscription list being more than twice that of any other library periodical in the world.

Current Biography also merits attention here.

This magazine, presenting articles on the life and work of people in the news, appears every month except in August, with a cumulated index to the previous issues of the current year. The sketches offer a summary of essential information — vital statistics, family background, education, career, and the like; references to other sources of material; a note on the pronunciation of difficult names; and photographic portraits.

About thirty men and women are chosen for presentation in each monthly issue. Only living personages are included, but brief obituary notices are printed upon the death of those who have already appeared in the magazine, with a citation to the earlier articles. "Who's News and Why," the magazine's subtitle, indicates the basis of selection in a generalized fashion. But people achieve fame, of course, in a variety of ways. They may personify in themselves a contemporary issue of importance, an explosive idea, a decisive trend in history; or they may acquire prominence, not so much as individuals, but as representatives of a significant body of opinion; or they may emerge into the spotlight after years of service behind the scenes by becoming involved in a single dramatic or meaningful incident. They are generally stable performers who, having gained renown in the past, can be reasonably expected to do so again in the future.

The selected "biographees" are interviewed by mail through a three-page multigraphed questionnaire that includes more than thirty queries, ranging from the influences that determined the subject's lifework to the color of his eyes. Almost all those who have appeared in the magazine have supplied some material for their sketches on this form. It is then turned over to a staff writer, along with any newspaper or magazine clippings collected in the office. The writer also receives a "research record" listing standard works like *Who's Who*. He must mark this sheet to indicate the sources consulted in preparing his article and thus, in effect, provides a check on his thoroughness. He is expected, however, to do additional probing on his own initiative.

The sketches, averaging fifteen hundred words in length, require two or three days of preparation. Kept as objective as possible, they follow a fairly established pattern. The first paragraph concisely identifies the biographee with a statement of his present title or position; the main body of the article consists of a narrative of his life, primarily in chronological order; and the final lines offer some personal details. At the end of the sketch is a list of source references.

On its completion, the manuscript is reviewed by the editors for accuracy, adherence to policy, and style. After its appearance in the monthly number, it is submitted to the subject for comments. It may then be revised to correct any errors and to bring it up to date with additional material and references before it reappears in the *Current Biography* yearbook, a compilation of all the sketches published during the year.

※　※　※

Thus the first fifty years . . .

The golden anniversary issue of the *Cumulative Book Index* in 1948 brought a host of congratulatory letters to the founder of the company. The writers urged him to look back upon his accomplishments "with justified pride"; they spoke of his "great vision and courageous enterprise"; they requested him to accept their "humble thanks"; they expressed the hope that he would enjoy many more years of "continued prosperity and well-being."

But doubtless Paul North Rice, president of the American Library Association, conveyed the appreciation of all librarians when he wrote, "It is really incredible that one man could do so much. We take your various indexes and bibliographies for granted, but when we think of what American libraries would do without them, we realize that it is not exaggeration to say that you have done more for libraries than any other living man."

These were tributes which even a modest man had to accept with deep satisfaction.

Part Two. The Present

CHAPTER VI

Compiling the CBI

Probably the greatest agony endured by a publisher is the belated discovery of errors in his books.

Wilson had his full share of this ordeal during the company's formative years. Neither he nor his editors could ever forget "The Church of the Early Bathers" and the other blunders. Seeking to prevent a repetition of such mistakes, he devised an elaborate set of precautions in the composing, handling, and checking of index copy. Refined over the years, these procedures are still used by the present staff to ensure completeness, promptness, and accuracy.

None of the individual methods will startle anyone familiar with the techniques of general publishing; but, in combination, they form a remarkable and perhaps unique process.

They are also highly involved.

Because of its complexity, the Wilson recipe for making an index cannot be dismissed in a few words. It will require two chapters: one for the *Cumulative Book Index* and one for the periodical indexes. As a unifying device, this first chapter will outline the *CBI* procedure from beginning to end in terms of a single book. But the reader ought to be cautioned that any discussion which isolates the processing of one book involves the usual risks of oversimplification. He should keep in mind, for example, that the *CBI* staff handles a multitude of books at the same time. Nor should he assume that the sequence to be outlined is always followed with exactness. Every book is processed in much the same way; but the order of processing may vary widely. The description here of the treatment accorded one volume must not obscure these two points.

✻ ✻ ✻

At an earlier stage of the company's history, every index editor had her own clerical staff. She was expected to borrow help from other editors according to her needs in meeting deadlines; but, naturally, none of them ever felt able to lend personnel — though, just as naturally, all of them sought aid on occasion. As a means of halting the resulting discord (as well as of isolating the indexers from the noisy clatter of typewriters), the production staffs of the *Cumulative Book Index* and seven periodical indexes were combined into one department, liaison between it and the editorial offices being maintained through the managing editors of the various publications.

This unified production force, numbering almost a hundred, is composed of six major units: a mail desk to record and direct the incoming flow of material; a compiling section for collecting and organizing that material; a section to check on names cited in the indexes; a central pool of typists for preparing copy for the printers; a group of "comparers" or copyreaders; and a smaller group of highly trained "revisers," whose duties are described below. All these units are under the direct command of a single production chief.

It was the mail desk of this department which, on July 18, 1946, received a mimeographed list of forthcoming books from the Viking Press of New York.

The clerk promptly delivered the list to the *Cumulative Book Index* editor, who turned it over to the compiling section. One of the members of this section then clipped information on each of the books from the publisher's sheet. Among the items was an announcement of a memoir of Franklin D. Roosevelt by Frances Perkins. No definite title or publication date was given; but the book was to be illustrated and was tentatively priced at $3.75.

This clipping, along with similar notices on other books, was filed alphabetically under the author's name in a cardboard box.

Two weeks later another report from the Viking Press stated that a title — "The Roosevelt I Knew" — had been selected and that publication of the book had been scheduled for November. On August 28, 1946, still another Viking list set the date of publication for November 1. Then, four weeks later, a catalog arrived from the Macmillan Company of Toronto which disclosed that it would release a Canadian edition (priced at $4.50) in November. All three clippings were attached to the original notice of the Perkins book.

At this point, it might be clarifying to repeat that eleven *CBI* numbers are printed annually. The January number covers a single month; the February number includes entries for both the current and the preceding month in one alphabet; the March number is again a single-month volume; and the April number "cumulates" the first four months. This cumulative sequence reoccurs throughout the year, with a semiannual number in July and an annual in December. Every five or six years, a "permanent" volume appears, incorporating entries for the entire period.

The Perkins memoir, of course, was set provisionally for the November 1946 number.

Preparation of copy for that number began on the first of the preceding month, with an editorial deadline for the twentieth. The book notices, first of all, were removed from the cardboard box in alphabetical groups, several letters being handled simultaneously. One of the compilers then checked through the notices to determine whether any of the books described in them had already been listed in an earlier number of the *CBI*. The search revealed, in the Perkins case, that this was a new work which had not been entered before. The clippings in regard to it, therefore, were pasted on a four-by-six-inch "authority" card, and the author's name was inscribed in the upper left-hand corner.

Now a preliminary check was made on the author's name.

The publisher's lists had identified Miss Perkins merely by her first and last names. Consulting various Wilson publications and other standard reference works, the investigator learned that Miss Perkins' married name was Mrs. Paul Wilson and that her birth year was 1882. Both these facts were added to the card.

It might then have been handled in one of three ways.

(1) If the book had been scheduled for publication at a much later date, the card would have been placed in a "Hold for Release" file. This collection is reviewed every month, and cards relating to books which will presumably be issued in time for the next *CBI* are withdrawn for further processing.

(2) If the information on the card had been inadequate, it would have been inserted into a "Send For" file, and an inquiry would have been dispatched to the Viking Press. Some eleven hundred such requests for information are sent every month. On the receipt of a satisfactory reply from the publisher or of additional material from other sources, the card would have been transferred to the "Hold for Release" file if the publication date was still distant; or, if the book was ready in time for the pending number of the *CBI*, the card would have been returned to the current working file.

(3) The Perkins card, however, went directly into the current file, for although its information was still relatively incomplete (and no assurance had been received as yet of the book's actual publication), the publisher's reputation for reliability made it certain that more material would soon be forthcoming.

Halsey W. Wilson shortly before the debut of the *Cumulative Book Index*, in 1898.

Justina (Leavitt) Wilson was her husband's "staff" when the *CBI* first appeared.

H. W. Wilson's bookstore in the basement of "Old Main" at the University of Minnesota, 1890 to 1900.

An early picture of the expanded staff that compiled the *Cumulative Book Index* and the *United States Catalog* (about 1900). (FRONT ROW, LEFT TO RIGHT) Florence McKay, Marion E. Potter, Emma Hart. (STANDING) Bertha Warner, Grace Lee, Nellie Frost, Bertha Tannehill, Amy Meader, Agnes Woollett, UNKNOWN

The H. W. Wilson Company's first building, erected in 1905 across from the main gateway to the University of Minnesota campus.

The New York City home of the Wilson company, on the banks of the Harlem River. The center unit, purchased in 1917, is flanked by larger wings added in 1929 and 1938. (This and succeeding photographs by Howard Kothe.)

The Wilson company Board of Directors today (LEFT TO RIGHT): Arthur Rigg; Charles J. Shaw, assistant to the president; Louis J. Bailey, chief librarian, Queens Borough Public Library; Howard Haycraft, vice-president; Edith M. Phelps, secretary; Marion E. Potter; and H. W. Wilson, president.

Looking south from the Wilson company roof, down Seventh Avenue, to Central Park and the Manhattan skyline.

The Wilson company editors and supervisors, May 1949.

(FRONT ROW, LEFT TO RIGHT) E. O. Erickson, head, Periodicals Department; E. Ethel Ashworth, head, Production Department; Margaret Furlong, editor, *Art Index;* Dorothy Charles, editor, *International Index.* Dorothy E. Cook, editor, *Standard Catalog Series;* Dorothy R. Carpenter, editor, *Education Index;* Marion E. Potter, editor, *Industrial Arts Index;* H. W. Wilson, president; Florence A. Arnold, editor, *Agricultural Index;* Mertice M. James, coeditor, *Book Review Digest;* Edward S. Kelley, superintendent, Printing and Binding departments.

(SECOND ROW, LEFT TO RIGHT) Dorothy H. West, editor, *Essay and General Literature Index;* Virginia Turrell, editor, *Bibliographic Index;* Sarita Robinson, editor, *Readers' Guide to Periodical Literature;* Anna H. Rothe, editor, *Current Biography;* Dorothy Brown, coeditor, *Book Re-*view Digest; E. Ethel Ashworth, head, Production Department; Margaret Furlong, editor, *Art Index;* Dorothy Charles, editor, *International Index.*

(BACK ROW, LEFT TO RIGHT) Marie D. Loizeaux, editor, *Wilson Library Bulletin;* Dorothy E. Cole, editor, *Library Literature;* John C. Evans, advertising manager; Florence D. Phin, editor, *Vertical File Service;* Howard Haycraft, vice-president; Marga Franck, editor, supplement to *Union List of Serials;* Charles J. Shaw, assistant to the president; Regina Goldman Grossman, editor, *Cumulative Book Index;* Arthur Rigg, head, Accounting Department; Bea Joseph, editor, *Biography Index;* John Jamieson, editor, general publications.

A corner of the Periodicals Clearing House, established by The Wilson Company to buy, store, and sell back-number copies. This department has grown into the largest business of its kind in the world, having a stock of some three million odd-number copies, a hundred thousand bound copies, and a thousand complete sets.

A partial view of the Production Department, where copy is prepared and proof checked for all the Wilson indexes.

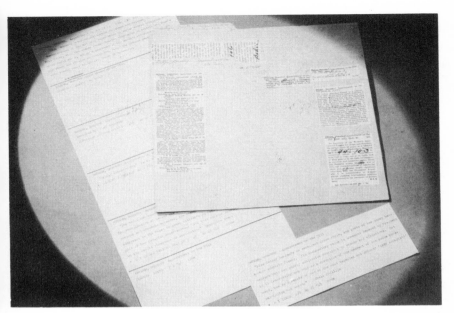

"Copy" for the *Book Review Digest*. (CENTER) One of the folders used for filing excerpts from reviews. (LEFT) A strip of copy paper on which annotations and excerpts are typed, one to a section. (LOWER RIGHT) A sample of a single section.

Interfiling linotype slugs to make "the metal catalog." Though the type must be read upside down, a trained worker can combine two alphabets of metal slugs faster than two sets of cards can be interfiled.

The Lighthouse is part of the Wilson story. Standing firmly upon a huge bronze book, the thirty-foot lighthouse, which is the Wilson colophon, symbolizes the guidance Wilson indexes give to those seeking their way through the maze of books and periodicals.

(*Below*) H. W. Wilson at his rolltop desk, 1949. Prominent on the desk's top are the rubber mice and bronze traps that symbolize the "better mousetrap" factor in the company's success. The ceramic cat on top of the books is the "oscar" presented to Mr. Wilson by the Special Libraries Association to commemorate the fiftieth anniversary of the *CBI* and the *United States Catalog,* which librarians familiarly call the "U.S. Cat."

Before filing the card, in fact, a *CBI* staff member conducted a search to discover whether that new material had not already appeared since the processing began. She found that a prepublication copy of the book itself had arrived in the interval — to be exact, on October 17, 1946.

Like the thousands of other books received by the company every year, it was subjected to a routine designed to make each copy serve a number of purposes. (This is done not only in fairness to the publishers, who furnish the books without charge, but also because of the company's own storage problems.) When *The Roosevelt I Knew* reached the mail desk of the Production Department, the clerk made out a book slip — an original and four duplicates — with a bibliographical description: author, title, size, paging, binding, publisher, price, and so forth. Accompanied by the five slips, the volume was then dispatched to the editor of the *Cumulative Book Index*. After a swift examination of the book, she marked the author and title on the original slip for separate entries in the index, since all books are automatically listed by author and almost all by title. She also noted subject headings — "Roosevelt, Franklin Delano" in this case — on the slip. It was then checked by a "reviser" and sent to the compiling section.

The book itself and the duplicate slips were directed to the company's library, whose staff retained two of the slips for their own use and delivered the remaining two to the editors of the *Standard Catalog Series* and the *Book Review Digest* for their information.

Returning to the *CBI* chronology: the original book slip was attached to the authority card, which, still moving in its alphabetical group, was inspected for completeness by the chief compiler and submitted to the *CBI* editor. The subject headings previously marked were checked again and further headings chosen if necessary. At the same time notes were made for any necessary "see also" references from related headings and "see" references from synonymous headings, to be included in the six-month and larger cumulations. (This process is described in greater detail in the next chapter.)

Then the card was returned to the Production Department.

On its arrival there, the names and vital statistics were verified and any missing data supplied by the "names section." Once more the company's own publications were the principal tools employed in this research, but other standard reference works in the section's extensive library were also used.

✗ ✗ ✗

At last, on the basis of the authority card, a typist prepared the following entries on a long sheet of paper, ruled to be cut later into three-by-six-and-a-half-inch slips (one entry per slip):

> PERKINS, FRANCES (MRS PAUL WILSON) 1882–
> Roosevelt I knew. O viii,408p il $3.75
> '46 Viking; $4.50 Macmillan (Toronto)
> ROOSEVELT, FRANKLIN DELANO, 1882–1945
> Perkins, F. Roosevelt I knew. $3.75 '46
> Viking; $4.50 Macmillan (Toronto)
> WILSON, MRS PAUL. See Perkins, F.

Since the title of the book in this instance began with the same word as the subject entry, a separate title entry was considered unnecessary. If there had been one, it would have read as follows:

> ROOSEVELT I knew. Perkins, F.
> $3.75 Viking; $4.50 Macmillan
> (Toronto)

The head of the revising section had this copy reviewed for correctness of form and checked against the authority card to eliminate transcribing errors.

It was then examined by a girl assigned to prepare a directory of publishers represented in the pending *CBI*. The "Publishers' Directory" appears in each number, for company names are abbreviated in the entries. Miss Perkins' publisher became simply "Viking," since the firm had published more than seven books listed in the *CBI*. If it had published fewer than seven, its complete name and address would have been stated in the entries.

The three Perkins entries were now cut into separate slips and filed alphabetically with other copy in preparation for the November number.

If anyone regards that second task as childishly simple, he might read the instructions that govern the work: "File copy word by word — first by main headings, then by subheads. If headings are identical, the following order will be observed: person, place, subject, title. In filing subheads, general subheads precede geographic concepts to make two separate alphabets under the main headings. Meetings (as subheads) are filed chronologically as separate alphabet before general subheads. Geological forms and time comprise separate alphabets filed after general subheads (see Webster for order). Under subhead History, periods are filed chronologically; but if two or more periods begin at the same date, the longer period is filed first. In filing names that are identical, the following order will be observed: Saints, Popes, Sovereigns, Princes and Others; forenames precede surnames and are followed by the compound forenames of each class mentioned above; Mr. precedes Mrs. of same surname; compound surnames follow simple ones; family names come last. In filing titles under . . ." Et cetera.

When all the copy in a letter group had been assembled it was inspected once again to remove or "scratch" any duplicate subject headings. In the Perkins entry, for example, the "Roosevelt, Franklin Delano" heading would have been eliminated if other entries having the same heading had been scheduled to appear before it in the November number. If, under those circumstances, it had not been "scratched," it would have been repeated in type since the printing department has orders to follow copy exactly as received. However, the heading was allowed to remain because the Perkins entry was the first to be listed under that classification.

Once this chore had been performed, the copy in that letter group was ready for the printer.

◾ ◾ ◾

Descending to the second-floor composing room, the alphabeted copy was divided into "takes" of one hundred and fifty printed lines. Identified as November *CBI* copy by initials and as a particular printing job by numbers, these "takes" were distributed among the dozen typesetting machines, which produce, on an average, about fifteen hundred lines each per shift.

Leaving the machines, the type slugs were placed in special sixteen-inch galley trays, closed at both ends and just wide enough to hold the lines. They were transported from one part of the printing department to another in steel trucks, which, fully loaded with more than a hundred trays, weigh over fifteen hundred pounds — a weight that requires the trucks to be equipped with special roller and ball-bearing wheels to permit easy movement.

Galley proofs were taken on a small hand press that holds a slug indicating the number of the truck and the name of the publication to which each galley belongs.

Then the proofs, accompanied by the copy, were sent to the Production Department.

A group of "comparers" there subjected them to a thorough scrutiny, seeking to ensure that the copy had been followed exactly and that the *CBI* style in margins, capitalization, type faces, and the like had been uniformly observed. If the copy itself appeared to be wrong, they consulted the chief reviser of the *CBI* — the only person in the Production Department (other than the head of the whole department) authorized to make copy changes. The comparers also checked on the alphabetical order; inspected the subject headings to be certain that all duplicates had been scratched; and signed their initials on the lower left-hand corner of each piece of copy. On the proofs, they indicated corrections in the margins as near the error as possible; noted the number of mistakes in a circle at the top; and signed their names to the first of each set of galleys examined by them. Then the proofs were sent back down to the printers, who reset the lines in which there were errors.

Four actions were taken on the revised galley proofs, printed in two sets on plain and gummed paper.

(1) The comparers read all the corrections, carefully checking the line above and below each of them for proper placement. If an error remained, they searched through the galley for the corrected line on the theory that it might have been inserted in the wrong place. If it could not be found, the mistake was marked again. The proofs were then "measured" — that is, the first word in each line of the revised galleys was compared with the first word of each line in the original galley — to prevent the loss or straying of any lines. The number of remaining errors was again noted at the top of both sets of galleys.

(2) The proofs were also read by the revisers to check on the form of the entries and to detect typographical mistakes, as well as by the editor of the CBI with special attention to the subject headings.

(3) Meanwhile, one of the revisers had been examining the file of material gathered since the processing of copy started. Any information of importance in this file was inserted directly on the proofs.

(4) Each entry on the gummed-paper set of proofs was then cut and pasted on the corresponding piece of copy. Since the slips had been arranged in the projected order of their appearance in the index, this procedure facilitated checking on the printer's arrangement of the type for the November number and later for the cumulations.

Once more the galley proofs were dispatched to the printing department.

After the ordered corrections had been made, the trucks of galley trays were rolled out to the make-up section. Here a veteran printer, trained from apprentice days to work on his feet, would have been astounded to see men sitting down to arrange the type in pages. They were seated before short-legged tables fitted with compartments for all the necessary tools and materials. On top of the table, at the make-up man's left, was a bank of shelves open at both ends, and beyond was the proof press. At his right was a truck of galleys. As soon as he completed a page, he slid it through one of the open shelves to the proof-press operator, who struck off a proof. Then the pages were placed in another truck and hauled away to be arranged in sixteen- or thirty-two-page forms.

While the printers handled this task, members of the Production Department were inspecting the page proofs.

The checkers had a whole set of instructions to guide their work: "Be sure to have the first page of front matter and main alphabet approved by the managing editor for date and volume number. . . . Read all corrections with care. . . . Mark faulty type and poor alignment of type. . . . Look for errors which might have been neglected in earlier processes. . . . Check runovers from page to page, continuity of page numbers, and the index's title line at the top of each page. . . . Get a revised proof of any page requiring difficult or complicated corrections. . . ."

After making the indicated changes, the printers locked the pages in the forms. Another proof was then taken — to be inspected only by the printing department in the case of regular numbers but also by the production staff on "permanent" volumes. Form trucks of the same height as the table on which the chases rested were brought alongside, and the chases were slid onto them and fastened in place. The truck tops were then tilted to a nearly vertical position to allow greater freedom of movement enroute to one of the seven large presses at the north end of the second floor.

On completion of the press-run, the pages were broken up and the type was replaced in galley trays to be stored for the next cumulated number of the *CBI*. (The storage racks, housed in a room at the rear of the building, where the base of a bluff rising behind the building provides a solid rock foundation, hold more than two hundred and fifty tons of live metal.)

The printed sheets of the catalog, meanwhile, had been transported to the bindery department, located on the floor directly above the large press room.

The sheets were there folded and assembled in proper order by special machines, sewed on wire stitchers, flattened to compress the bulky pages, trimmed by a giant razor-sharp blade, glued, bound, and mailed to the eight thousand subscribers all over the world — reaching the great majority of them early in November. Since these were single-month copies, the task seemed comparatively simple to the bindery workers. They could remember the huge 1928 edition of the *United States Catalog*, which was 3164 folio-size pages thick and weighed twenty-seven pounds.

One of the first available copies of the completed issue was promptly examined by the *CBI* staff.

Each entry was compared with the authority cards, and mistakes that had escaped detection in the earlier readings — and, surprisingly, some always do — were corrected on the printed pages. Significant data collected since the last galley proofs were also added to make this "correction" copy one of the primary sources of material for the next cumulated number. In the case of the Perkins memoir, the company had received a Library of Congress catalog card for the book, and its serial number was transferred to the "correction" copy. The symbol (W), indicating that "Wilson cards" (see page 71) had been made for the book, was also inserted. When work began on the next cumulative

number, these changes, plus the new entries, were typed onto the long sheets for the editorial processing already described. (The technique of combining new and old entries
will be outlined in the next chapter.)

Yet work on the Perkins entries was not ended.

Early in 1947 a notice arrived that an English edition had
been published in London at eighteen shillings by the firm
of Hammond. The original entries, incorporating this new
information, were then reprinted in the current *CBI* number.

Still later changes or additions, if any, could be inserted
up to and including the permanent six-year (1943–1948)
cumulation.

⋈ ⋈ ⋈

It might be wise at this point to repeat the warning issued
at the beginning of this chapter.

The concentration on the Perkins volume has been a literary device to simplify the discussion; but it will have been
more misleading than useful if the reader forgets that this
was only one book among hundreds of others.

Yet an accurate picture of the work cannot be achieved
merely by multiplying the actions taken in regard to the
Perkins book, for the order of processing may be different
on each volume. The arrival of the first notice from the
Viking Press started the processing on the Perkins memoir.
But it might have started with the receipt of the book itself — or the book might not have arrived until long after
the *CBI* had noted (on the basis of other reliable information) its publication. *The Roosevelt I Knew* appeared first
in the United States, then in Canada, and later in England;
but, of course, the sequence might have been reversed. Miss
Perkins' book was also published in time to be entered in a
single-month number of the *CBI*; if it had been scheduled
for a cumulative number, the entries for it would have become involved in a more complex processing.

All these variations in events would have changed the

chronology of the procedures described here — though usually not the procedures themselves. If this makes the work of the *CBI* staff appear infinitely complicated, then the correct impression has been created. For it *is* infinitely complicated.

CHAPTER VII

The Periodical Indexes

It will surprise no one that a report on the compiling of the periodical indexes must begin with the periodicals themselves.

Like the books for the *CBI*, the magazines are supplied without charge by the publishers, who recognize that a listing in a Wilson index will not only prolong the life of a periodical, but substantially increase its library circulation.

Every publication sent to the company, however, is not automatically entered in an index. The chosen ones are selected, in accordance with long-standing policy, by a vote of the subscribers to each index. Polls are conducted at regular intervals to determine which periodicals, in the opinion of the subscribers, have the greatest reference value. Mere popularity is not enough to justify acceptance; some widely circulated magazines have relatively little worth as sources of research material. The voters also have to consider the problem of balance. Since the indexes are necessarily limited in size, the inclusion of too many journals in one field may mean the exclusion of some other field entirely.

The magazines, like the books, are handled on arrival at the company by the mail desk of the Production Department. They are there checked off on a record of all the incoming periodicals surveyed by the indexes. Then, speed being essential, they are rushed at once to the editors.

ᴝ ᴝ ᴝ

Before outlining the indexing procedures, the problem of subject headings must be considered.

During the early days of the company, the editors had few guides to subject-entry form. The American Library Association had published a slender list of generalized headings, and the Peabody and Athenaeum catalogs were available; but these did not always agree. The result was a friendly dispute among the staff members of the indexes. Miss Guthrie, then editor of the *Readers' Guide,* preferred the straight Peabody headings ("Child Labor"), while Miss Potter favored the Athenaeum's subdivisions ("Children — Employment"). The discussion continued until in time the two editors had converted each other. Then it was resumed with Miss Guthrie defending Miss Potter's former position and Miss Potter advocating Miss Guthrie's discarded theories.

The lack of adequate bibliographic tools increased the difficulty of the work and made the factor of time even more important. Consequently, haste being necessary, the editors had to depend upon titles as a guide to classifying — a guide that was often unreliable. A volume entitled *Ancient Labor* was once tentatively classified under "Labor and laboring classes"; but the indexer followed a hunch and, inspecting the book more closely, discovered it to be a treatise on obstetrics.

The University of Minnesota faculty was helpful in the first years. The professors might know little of library subject headings, but they knew a great deal about their own special fields. Miss Potter was constantly seeking their advice. "What about 'contagious diseases'?" she would ask the startled head of the medical school; "or should it be 'infectious diseases,' or perhaps 'communicable diseases'?" But this was a time-consuming, even though highly dependable, method of checking on subject headings.

Conditions have changed drastically since that time. Today the editors have at their command such tools as the *Public Affairs Information Service*, encyclopedias, medical indexes, chemical abstracts, handbooks, textbooks, Library of Congress publications, and a multitude of others — including the Wilson company's own indexes. Yet, despite half a century of progress in library science, the selection of subject headings remains the indexers' most perplexing problem.

The choice is based on a number of factors.

It is dictated primarily by common usage, since the editors want to produce indexes that will answer the ordinary man's inquiries with a minimum of trouble. The headings, in other words, must be the ones the library patron himself might use. But accuracy is also a factor.

The attainment of accuracy, of course, can be difficult even when that quality alone is the objective; it can verge on the impossible at times if the emphasis has been placed on common usage. "Moving pictures," for example, is not strictly accurate; but since most people are familiar with that term, the editors have been obliged to use it instead of the more precise heading, "motion pictures."

As a further means of helping the average researcher, the indexers attempt to keep related subjects as near each other in the alphabet as possible. This is often accomplished, as was mentioned earlier, by inverting the headings so as to bring related references together. Thus "military service, compulsory" puts material on that issue with other military headings; the alternative heading of "conscription" would separate them.

But this policy creates additional problems. "Personnel manager" is a much more accepted term today than "employment manager," but the editors of the *Industrial Arts Index* employ the latter so that all their material on employment can be assembled in one place. The policy also raises questions about which part of a heading should be regarded as the most important. The answer must take into account the nature of the index. Thus the *Industrial Arts* editors use "education of workers" in the belief that the education part is more important to their readers than the second part. On the other hand, the editors of *Education Index*, which is entirely concerned with education, stress the opposite thought by using "workers — education."

Every index also has its own special difficulties in assigning subject headings.

Miss Potter and her associates on the *Industrial Arts* must have at least a nodding acquaintance with the peculiar jargon of a dozen or more scientific fields. This intimacy is not easily achieved or maintained. Physics, for example, has developed almost a whole new vocabulary in recent years. Liquid helium posed a typical problem. What heading should be used for it? Since it has been called "a second sound," some indexers place it in the category of "sound"; others insist that "heat waves" would be a more satisfactory classification.

Faced with a set of competing terms, moreover, the *Industrial Arts* editors must sometimes have a prophetic eye for the one which will survive in common usage. When DDT was first produced, countless articles appeared in which several names and terms were used for it. The chemical name, dichlorodiphenyltrichloroethane, had the advantage of being accurate; but who, except a few learned chemists, would know it? The *Industrial Arts* staff decided to use DDT — a "reasoned guess" that has proved sound, for the insecticide is now known only by that name.

The *Education Index* also has its troubles. Most of them arise out of confusing terminology. "General education," for example, may mean a kind of liberal arts education; or it may mean education for less able students. Similarly, on the *International Index*, "values" may be interpreted by a psychology review as preferences, but a philosophy journal may translate the term as a measure of worth.

The plight of the *Biography Index*, though not strictly a periodical index, might also be mentioned here. This publication, containing an index by occupation (as well as a main alphabet of names), would seem to present few problems. But how should a man who intermittently holds political office be classified in it? He might be regarded as a "statesman"; but perhaps his past achievements and present status do not justify so lofty a title. "Public servant" might be equally inappropriate for the same reasons. He could be placed in the category of his office; or if recently removed from power, he might still be identified as, say, an ex-prime minister. But what if he has not been in office for some time? The first-thought answer would be "politician." This, unfortunately, is a nasty word. According to standard dictionaries, a politician may be one who seeks or conducts public office for party ends or personal advantage. Nor is "politico" an acceptable alternative, for that term has offensive connotations in Latin America. The *Biography Index* editors have never succeeded in finding the right word. (Suggestions will be welcomed.) They have been obliged to evade the issue by connecting the political personage with his current or former title and, in a few cases, using the "statesman" category.

They have triumphantly survived another crisis, however. What was Magda Lupescu's profession? It would be fairly simple to propose several, and most of them would be libelous. The editors were considering the merits of filing her under "Favorites, Royal," when the lady obligingly legalized her status by a "death-bed" marriage to ex-King Carol — recovering from her illness shortly thereafter.

Almost all of the indexes — and especially Miss Potter's *Industrial Arts* — are beset with subject-heading difficulties which result from their constantly expanding size. As more magazines are added, the need for more detailed indexing increases. The small index can put several scattered articles on plastics, for example, under that simple heading. But when two magazines devoted exclusively to plastics are to be indexed, as in the *Industrial Arts Index*, the number of entries would become unwieldy if all were assigned to a single category. Consequently, the editors must investigate the various aspects of plastics to be able to use more specific headings.

The same pattern can be observed in comparing two different indexes. The *Abridged Readers' Guide* can list under "education" virtually every relevant article in its thirty-odd magazines; but, of course, the *Education Index* needs hundreds of subdivisions to cover the same field.

The problems do not end even after a subject heading has been chosen.

Common usage changes over the years: the "wireless telephone" becomes the "radio." At a later date, too, the editors may be able to adopt a more accurate heading. "Gas and oil engines" was once a favorite term; and, since engines cannot be both gas *and* oil, it was also a misleading one. As mechanical knowledge spread, the indexers could substitute "internal combustion engines," a classification which includes not only gas and oil, but the modern Diesel engines as well. Changing to another term may also become desirable because it will permit a unification of the several related headings.

Yet changes are never ordered without due reflection. Many librarians rely on the Wilson indexes for guidance in the selection of subject headings for their own card catalogs. It might be comparatively simple for the company to change; but the librarians could not do so without a costly revision of their files.

The editors, therefore, are frequently faced with a dilemma: if they discard obsolete headings, the librarians may suffer; and if they do not discard them, the user may be penalized. There is not, and cannot be, an easy formula for resolving this conflict of duties. Miss Potter was once asked about her policy in regard to outmoded headings. "When I shudder at them and can't stand them any longer," she replied, "I finally change them."

✖ ✖ ✖

For the purposes of clarity, the ensuing discussion of indexing procedures will be limited to the unabridged *Readers' Guide to Periodical Literature.*

This index, covering some hundred and seventeen magazines, is published semimonthly from September through June and monthly in July and August. Because of that schedule, it must be compiled with remarkable dispatch. The editorial deadline for the first of the monthly issues is the first Friday of the month, and by that day all magazines on hand in the Wilson office must have been indexed. (A few late arrivals are indexed on Monday.) The mechanical processing of copy requires another week. Thus by the following Friday the *Guide* is in the mail on its way to the subscribers. In order to facilitate the indexing, some of the weekly magazines provide advance proof sheets or arrange for a special delivery by messenger, so that on occasion the *Guide* has reached a library ahead of some of the magazines themselves.

Three editors, each examining from four to six periodicals a day, handle the indexing. This is in addition, of course, to the reading of proofs — a chore which, again because of the demand for speed, has top priority over all other work. The magazines are usually divided among the staff according to kind, enabling a single person to process related material. However, the informal arrangement can be abandoned under pressure because each editor has been trained to index any magazine, regardless of its content. The publications are not read in detail, but scanned quickly. Nor are all the articles indexed. The *Guide* is not intended to be a full index of the periodicals or an abstract of all their articles; as its title indicates, it is merely a guide.

Though librarians would be appalled to witness such defacing, the editors mark up the magazines thoroughly by penciling subject headings and references around the articles. When margins are small and headings numerous, this can be a hard task for an indexer rushing to get a periodical off her desk — as well as for the typist who has to prepare copy from the notes under similar stress.

Ordinarily the title of an article will state or suggest its subject and can be simply repeated in the index. But when it is confusing or uninformative, the indexers must make an addition to it. Thus the purpose of an article called "As Pretty Does" would be clarified by adding the words, "Planning a table setting." Then the proper subject headings are written next to the title.

As far as possible, the *Guide* adopts the headings used by the Library of Congress or other standard sources. But since these were devised for book cataloging, they are not always specific enough for magazine articles. Indeed, they may not suggest *any* heading for certain contemporary topics. When articles began appearing, for instance, on the conference between Molotov and the Western Powers in regard to the Berlin crisis, the standard sources offered no help in selecting a subject heading for them, and an official title for the parleys had not been announced. After due deliberation, the *Guide* editors indexed the stories under "Moscow Conferences — 1948."

At this point, cross-references may be added to the marked-up magazine. The "see also" references direct the reader to other material related to the subject of the article. (Thus: Desserts, frozen; see also Ice cream, ices, etc.) The "see" references direct the reader from alternative forms of personal names or subject headings to the authorized forms used by the *Guide*. (Thus: Petroleum as fuel; see Oil fuel.) The "see also" references are held out of the smaller paper-bound numbers and are inserted only in the major cumulations. Records are maintained of their use; and if they have appeared in a previous number since the last bound volume, they are not repeated. For it should always be remembered that the *Guide*, like most of the Wilson indexes, is a continuing publication; the paper-bound numbers must not be regarded as separate units. Consequently, for the "see also" references a user is expected to consult not only the latest issue but all the earlier paper-covered cumulations since the last bound volume.

After being indexed, the magazines are sent out to the Production Department.

※   ※   ※

The typists prepare copy from the periodicals on long sheets of paper, tagging a line to the name entries to help the names section in identifying them. (James F. Byrnes, for example, would be labeled as a former U.S. Secretary of State.) After serving their purpose, these lines are removed from the copy so the linotype operators will not set them.

The copy is inspected by "revisers" for accuracy in transcribing and conformity to style before being submitted to the managing editor of the index for a second review. The managing editor scrutinizes such details as titles, paging, and dates; and she re-examines the subject headings and references.

Returned to the Production Department, the copy sheets are then cut into separate slips, one entry to each slip, and these are filed in alphabetical order.

When a sufficient number of slips have been collected to permit efficient operation, the name entries are removed and dispatched to the names staff. Its five members search through earlier Wilson indexes to determine whether the names have been cited before; if so, the previous spelling and vital statistics are considered authoritative. If the initial search proves fruitless, the staff turns to other standard reference works. The index's managing editor, meanwhile, has been "scratching" duplicate subject headings. (This action has been described in connection with the processing of *CBI* material.)

On being sent back to the Production Department, the two sections — the names and the subject entries — are once more combined in a single alphabet. They are then delivered, in groups of two or three letters at a time, to the printers. The flow of copy is carefully regulated to maintain a monthly schedule compiled in advance by the chief of the Production Department in consultation with all the index editors and the printing superintendent. It is designed not only to produce the indexes on time, but to ensure a steady use of the available linotype machines.

The first proofs are subjected to a routine inspection by "comparers," who check the printed lines against the typewritten copy.

The second proofs, revised to eliminate the previous errors, are returned in two sets. One is printed on the regular plain galley sheets; the other on gummed paper. (The use of the latter will be considered in the next section.) The plain galleys are checked again to guarantee that all the earlier mistakes have been corrected and to guard against the introduction of any new ones. They are then "measured" — which means, as the reader will remember, that each line in the revised galleys is compared with the first word of each line in the original galleys. This is intended to prevent the loss or straying of a line.

Both the alphabeted slips of copy and the revised proofs are then turned over to the index editors for another editorial reading. Following this review, the proofs are sent, via the Production Department, to the printers. When the type has been assembled in page form, further proofs are pulled. These pages are "measured" against the revised galley proofs, and comparers read them to make sure that the ordered corrections have been made.

Then, after a final check on the "form proofs" by the printers, the *Readers' Guide* is ready for the press.

❧ ❧ ❧

The foregoing outline refers to single numbers containing only new material. The process is somewhat different on cumulated numbers which combine both new and old entries.

The second or revised galley proofs, as already noted, are printed in two sets: one on plain and another on gummed paper. The plain sets are used for editorial and typographical corrections; but the gummed sets are clipped and each entry is pasted on the corresponding piece of copy. This "pasted copy" serves later as a guide in the combining of new and old type.

New copy for a cumulated number is prepared, typed, cut into separate slips, and alphabeted — all in the customary manner. As usual, too, the name entries are removed for checking by the names section. The remaining subject entries are submitted to the index's managing editors, who "scratch" the duplicate headings. On a cumulated number, this entails a review of both the new copy and the past numbers to be combined, for the editors must eliminate from the copy all headings that appear there more than once or that have already appeared in the earlier numbers.

The subject copy is returned to the Production Department to be reunited with the name entries.

Since the half-line "see also" references, the regular six-point type, and the agate lines must be set on different linotype machines, the copy is sent to the printers in three separate alphabets. The copy flow must be so arranged, however, that entries in each of these alphabets are dispatched with the same letter group in the other two alphabets. Thus the agate lines in the "A" group must accompany the reference and text lines of that group.

At the same time, the Production Department is handling still another kind of copy. During the interval between the index's last number and its forthcoming cumulation, the editors have been marking, directly in the index, all the errors that escaped earlier detection. These are typed onto the usual long sheets, identified as "line corrections," cut into separate entries, filed in alphabetical order, and delivered to the printing department with the rest of the new material for the combined number.

The first proofs of these various alphabets are subjected to the routine checks and returned to the printers.

The revised proofs are printed on gummed paper only. After these have been read in the Production Department, each entry is cut and pasted onto the appropriate piece of copy—with a single exception. The line corrections are clipped, not pasted, since they are to be transferred later to the original copy slips.

This pasted-up copy—still in separate alphabets ("see also," main, agate, etc.)—is returned to the printing department where it serves as an aid in the combining of new and old type.

Specially trained women seated at steel tables handle the task of interfiling the metal linotype slugs. Type, as stated earlier, can be combined much faster than catalog cards. In the latter case, the librarian must finger through the old cards to locate the right place for a new one. With type, the combiner has only to glance down the galley to find where the added entry should be inserted. Of course, the fact that the type must be read upside down creates an initial difficulty; but this obstacle can be overcome by practice. With two alphabets of type to combine, the average Wilson worker can assemble as many as a hundred galleys—about six thousand entries—in an eight-hour shift.

Proofs are taken of the combined galleys and submitted to the Production Department.

Two steps are taken there as a precaution against errors. First, the "correction" copy of the earlier number is reviewed to make sure that every mistake noted in its pages has been corrected in the proofs. Then, just as the printers combined the new and old type, the Production Department staff interfiles the new and old slips of copy.

Using this file as a guide, they carefully examine the combined galleys. One member of a team holds the copy and reads aloud "in a low voice" (according to instructions) the first word of each line. The other member, holding the proofs, in effect answers "present" or "absent" for the lines. The magnitude of this chore is sometimes staggering, particularly on a cumulation like the two-year *Readers' Guide*. That number must contain, at a rough estimate, about four hundred thousand lines. The roll call not only reveals the disappearance of a line or mistakes in the alphabetical order; it also provides an opportunity for checking again on the corrections, since these are clipped to each piece of copy on which a change was to be made.

On larger cumulations (semiannual, annual, etc.), two additional readings are made of the galleys.

The first is performed by the Production Department. It is concerned largely with details: paging, titles, volume numbers, dates, combinations, and similar matters. The skill with which this is done can only be acquired through experience. If, for example, someone has been checking entries from a certain periodical for some time and has observed that all of them refer to Volume 91, he will naturally be suspicious on encountering a reference to Volume 19 of the same magazine.

The second reading is conducted by the index editors. This is an over-all check. It might disclose, for instance, that an unwieldy number of entries has been placed under a broad subject heading. The editors will then add more specific headings or subdivisions to permit the entries to be separated into smaller and more convenient categories.

The rest of the process of handling cumulations is identical with that used in single numbers. However, in "permanent" volumes, a further check is made in the Production

Department of the form proofs, which ordinarily are inspected only by the printing staff.

※ ※ ※

This report on the processing of copy for the periodical indexes must close with a confession — a confession of several sins of omission.

The step-by-step analysis, first of all, may well have created a false impression. The reality does not conform to such a simple pattern. For the sake of clarity, some order has been imposed on a scene of apparent chaos; but it should not be supposed that the same sort of order exists in fact. Many of the processes, here described as occurring in sequence, are actually simultaneous: magazines are indexed, subject copy scratched, names searched, proofs read — all at the same time and on all the indexes.

Nor has this discussion even mentioned some of the annoying little details which harass the editorial staffs. As an illustration, one might consider the plight of the *Art Index* editor with respect to architects. "These gentlemen," she once said with a resigned air, "present one of our biggest problems. We index a large number of periodicals, which involves trying to get accurate information about all types of architects. I say trying, because architects aren't easy to locate; the younger ones aren't usually listed in *Who's Who*, and since a large number don't belong to the American Institute of Architects, they don't appear in the *Annuary* which that body publishes. Furthermore, they don't ever sit still! One year they work alone and the next year they turn up as 'joint' architects, or members of an architectural firm. Sometimes two firms work on the same project. Since we make 'see also' references from every firm to every member of that firm and cross-references from one 'joint' architect to another, it is easy to see how complicated the references might become." And, of course, every index has similar problems.

Finally, by its cautious pace, this outline may have suggested that the work of indexing and copy-processing advances with equal slowness. Nothing could be more remote from the truth.

Some realization of the pace may be gained by submitting a full calendar of the *Readers' Guide* deadlines.

The *Guide*, it should be recalled, is published on a semi-monthly schedule. Two weeks are spent on the indexing, and on Friday of the second week this task must be completed. By nightfall on Monday, the copy must be prepared, revised, checked, alphabeted, and delivered to the printers. The linotype operators work through the night, and early on Tuesday morning a stack of proofs is waiting for processing in the Production Department. By Wednesday noon all the proofs are ready. Before the end of that day, three things have to be accomplished: all the proofs must be returned to the printing department; most of the new type must be combined with the old; and many pages of the first part of the alphabet must be read. The entire issue is printed on Thursday. On Friday, the eighty-five hundred copies are bound, packaged, and sent off to the post office.

Though not all the indexes have such a punishing schedule, none of the editors can afford to dawdle. They are racing with the clock in a contest they cannot afford to lose. Since all of them are women, their constant victory deals another blow to that ancient dictum about the weaker sex.

CHAPTER VIII

The Service Basis

Although the point ought to be obvious by now, it must be repeated that bibliographic publishing is an extremely hazardous adventure.

Sales have always been limited; costs are high; and the financial risks have to be borne for extended periods before any return whatsoever, much less a decent profit, can be realized on the investment.

These facts alone would be sufficient to discourage most prudent men. But bibliographers can seldom be accused of prudence, and some students have been sorely tempted to consider them a race apart. Wilson cannot be regarded as an exception. He was fortunate, however, in having a wide background of practical experience. He had acquired a deep respect — but no veneration — for the dollar sign in business transactions while earning his way through school; he had gained a knowledge of printing through the operation of his "bedroom" press; and, being the owner of a bookstore, he had been obliged to master the art of management. As a result, he was a thorough realist at the age of thirty.

But it is highly doubtful whether he could have succeeded where so many others had failed without the "service basis." The origin of that device has already been described; but the fundamental convictions upon which it rests must be re-emphasized. Examining the record of past failures, Wilson reached a number of conclusions. He decided that the cooperative method of indexing was in itself an almost fatal defect. As the initial enthusiasm of the volunteers subsided, the project was certain to be impeded by defections which weakened the continuity of its leadership, aggravated its administrative problems, multiplied its financial burdens, and in time brought about its collapse.

Even when the cooperating agencies resolutely supported an indexing venture, it often failed for another reason. Large libraries, with vast book and periodical holdings, insistently urged an expanded service. The costly attempt to satisfy their demands set off a disastrous chain reaction: the small libraries, unable to afford the higher prices, canceled their orders; the reduction in the number of subscribers boosted costs; the resulting increase in rates compelled still others to retire; and the vicious circle continued until even the wealthiest patrons found the service beyond their means.

Wilson was familiar with this circle in his own business. Durng his company's experimental years, he was confronted with a deficit that became more and more alarming. Nonetheless, though his indexes were already losing money, some of the subscribers complained of their inadequacy while others protested their cost.

But how could every user receive precisely the service he wanted at a price within his budget?

Wilson thought for a time that the scheme of printing each entry on a separate card might be an ideal solution; but on further study he decided that the assumption that this would be more economical was false. On the contrary, it would have proved far more expensive, because it not only would have required an elaborate distribution system for processing orders, but would have failed to reduce the basic costs of production.

Obviously, the service demanded by the largest customer

determined the two principal items in the publisher's account books: editorial and typesetting costs. Once performed for a big library, the editorial work need not be done again for the small patron; once assembled for all the necessary entries, the type could be used repeatedly. The subscriber with minimum needs, in other words, increased production costs only to the extent of the actual printing, binding, and distribution costs of his own copy of an index. Consequently, if he paid these latter costs, he could not be regarded as a burden on those who preferred the complete service. If he paid more than these costs, he made a contribution toward the editorial and composition expenses and thus permitted a reduction in the price charged to the purchaser of the whole service.

Admittedly, he should make some contribution; but, according to Wilson, he should do so in proportion to the amount of service used. For the sake of justice, he could not be expected to pay a flat fee computed by dividing the total production costs by the number of subscribers. If asked to do so, he would have no choice except to withdraw, and the loss of his support could only mean an increase in the rates charged to those who remained, thus beginning the old vicious circle again.

Any analysis of the Wilson pricing system must stress one point above all others.

The company insists that a subscriber is not buying a book or a periodical, but an indexing *service* which just happens to appear in book or periodical form. If the service were delivered on catalog cards, a library would order and expect to pay only for those which applied to its own collection. But the fact that the cards are printed in page form for convenience and economy does not really alter the situation. Each customer is still receiving the entries he needs; and only those he needs are valuable to him. Each, therefore, ought to be prepared to pay accordingly.

"It would be quite as fair," the company s favorite analogy

reads, "to charge each customer the same amount per month for electricity, regardless of the current used, as to demand equal support for indexes from the village library and the metropolitan institution." One must hastily add, in order to avoid any misunderstanding, that the vital difference between the village and the metropolitan library is not in their relative ability to pay; it is in the varying degree of service which they derive from the indexes.

But, granting this contention, how is the service to be metered with accuracy?

𝕄   𝕄   𝕄

Of the two methods employed in translating theory into practice, the first and somewhat simpler one concerns the periodical indexes.

The price charged for any of these publications is determined on the basis of the number of indexed periodicals received by each library. Thus, while each subscriber receives the complete index, he pays only for the indexing of those magazines taken by his institution — that is, for the service he actually uses as determined by periodic checklists of his holdings.

It should be repeated here that the periodicals to be indexed are selected by a poll of the subscribers to each index. This is no mere "popularity contest." On the contrary, the questionnaires sent out for this purpose every few years request each subscriber to vote thoughtfully "Yes" or "No" on the *reference value* of each periodical that he receives, whether newly proposed for inclusion or already indexed. As a result of the balloting, a magazine may well be dropped, sometimes after years of continuous indexing, if its character has changed and its reference value diminished. Conversely, certain highly popular periodicals with low reference value have tried for years to be elected but without success. A recent *Readers' Guide* poll, for example, disclosed that a woman's fashion magazine was received by forty-one per cent of the subscribers — who, nonetheless, voted two to one *against* its inclusion. For some of the indexes the voting questionnaire and the checklist for recording a library's holdings are combined in a single form; on other indexes separate forms are used.

For rate-setting purposes, the periodical indexes are divided into two groups: the *Readers' Guide to Periodical Literature* and its abridged edition in the first class; and the specialized indexes, like the *Art Index* and the *Education Index*, in the second.

Actually, the same basic principles apply to both groups. The differences are mainly procedural. The determining factors in establishing the cost for indexing a periodical in either group are: (1) the number of entries required per year to index the periodical — sometimes referred to as the difficulty of indexing; and (2) the number of subscribers taking that periodical — that is, the number among whom the cost of indexing may be divided.

For most of the periodicals indexed in the unabridged edition of the *Readers' Guide*, the amount of variation in the two factors is relatively slight. The little that does exist is compensated for by a sliding scale of charges. Thus, as the periodicals become more scholarly and difficult to index (and with fewer libraries to share the cost of indexing), a moderately higher charge is made to the subscribers:

1–80 periodicals .... 40¢ each (minimum rate: $12)

81–100 periodicals .... 50¢ each

Over 100 periodicals .... 60¢ each

The subscription price to a given library is ascertained by applying the above scale to the number of indexed periodicals received by that library. For example: a library receiving 50 indexed periodicals will pay $20 (50 periodicals at 40¢ each); a library receiving 90 periodicals will pay $37 (80 at 40¢ each, 10 at 50¢ each); and a library receiving all of the 113 periodicals for which a charge is made at present will pay $49.80 (80 at 40¢ each, 20 at 50¢ each, and 13 at 60¢ each). A library taking fewer than 30 periodicals will pay the minimum rate of $12, which ensures an adequate contribution toward total production costs by every subscriber. (Or such a library has the option of transferring its subscription to the smaller abridged edition.)

Since the thirty-five magazines currently indexed in the *Abridged Readers' Guide* (designed for smaller libraries) are virtually equal in popularity and similar in nature, the pricing is even simpler: a straight 40¢ per periodical, with a minimum subscription rate of $3.60 — which, as already stated, ensures an adequate contribution to production costs by each subscriber.

The price yardstick on the specialized indexes (*Art, International, Education, Agricultural, Industrial Arts*, etc.) is a more complex instrument. Perhaps the computing procedures can be best outlined in terms of a recent revision of the *Art Index* rates. It was necessary, first of all, to determine the cost of indexing a single entry. This was accomplished by dividing the current annual cost of making the *Art Index* ($42,281) by the current annual number of entries (32,393); the result was a basic cost-per-entry of $1.30.

Then the charge-per-subscriber for each indexed periodical had to be discovered. This involved two major steps. The total number of entries required to index a given magazine for one year was multiplied by the basic cost-per-entry to find the total annual cost of indexing that magazine. This, in turn, was divided by the number of libraries which had checked that magazine on the current checklists to establish the charge for each of its subscribers. Naturally, the resulting range of prices was tremendous. The *Formes et Couleurs* of Paris, requiring more than five hundred entries but taken by only thirty-six libraries, cost each of them almost twenty dollars on their *Art Index* bills. But the *Museum of Modern Art Bulletin*, with only forty-seven entries, added a mere twenty-three cents to the subscription price of the more than two hundred libraries which received it.

The full subscription rate for any subscriber, of course, was the sum of the charges for those magazines checked by him — unless the amount was less than twelve dollars, in which case that minimum charge appeared on his account.

After a library has subscribed for a first copy of any Wilson periodical index at its checklist rate, it is entitled to subscribe for additional copies of the same index — *for use in the same library* — at the minimum rate. All branch or departmental libraries of large systems (except purely subsidiary divisions under the same roof as the main library) pay individual first-copy rates based on checklists of *their own* periodical holdings, i.e., in proportion to their own use. Only in this way is the company able to treat all systems uniformly; financial and administrative practices and geographical distinctions vary so widely between institutions that attempts in the past to base an additional-copy policy on such factors resulted in grave inequities.

⚮ ⚮ ⚮

The service basis is applied to the "book indexes" (the *Cumulative Book Index, Book Review Digest, Standard Catalog Series*, etc.) in a somewhat different manner.

For these publications, the price yardstick is the average annual sum spent by a library for books and periodicals, exclusive of binding, over a period of three years. Since setting a special rate for every minute variation in the funds would be manifestly impossible, the company has compromised on a scale of fourteen classes. The 1948–49 scale is reproduced on page 122. It will be apparent at once that the prices do not increase in exact ratio to the mounting size of the expenditures. The rate paid for the *Cumulative Book Index* by a library in Class 1, with an annual expenditure of less than two hundred dollars, is ten dollars. But the charge assigned to a Class 14 library, with expenditures eight hundred times greater, is not eight hundred times the minimum price; it is, instead, only ninety dollars. This is another compromise which, in the company's opinion, benefits the larger libraries without injuring the smaller ones.

SERVICE BASIS RATE SCALE, 1948–49

CLASS	1	2	3	4	5	6	7	8	9	10	11	12	13	14
Book & periodical expenditures:	under $200	$200-300	$300-500	$500-800	$800-1,300	$1,300-2,000	$2,000-3,200	$3,200-5,000	$5,000-10,000	$10,000-20,000	$20,000-40,000	$40,000-80,000	$80,000-100,000	over $100,000
Cumulative Book Index ..	$10	12	13	16	21	26	32	38	44	52	63	72	81	90
Book Review Digest	$5	6	7	8	10	12	14	16	18	20	22	24	26	28
Essay Index	$5	5	5	5	6	8	10	12	14	16	20	24	30	36
Vertical File Service	$4	4	4	4	5	6	7	8	9	10	10	10	10	10
Bibliographic Index	$6	6	6	7	8	10	12	14	16	19	22	25	28	32
*Library Literature	$4	4	4	5	6	8	10	12	14	16	18	20	22	24
Current Biog. Yrbook ...	$5	5	5	5	6	7	8	9	10	11	11	11	11	11
Biography Index	$4	5	6	7	8	10	12	14	16	18	20	22	24	26

* Except library schools, which pay for this publication on a special basis.

The scale published here is designed for public, college, university, normal school, state, and institutional libraries. It does *not* apply to elementary and high schools, or to booksellers, publishers, and individuals. School libraries are rated by school enrollment, not by library funds. (The charges are generally lower than those on the accompanying scale, except for the *Standard Catalog for High School Libraries* and the *Children's Catalog,* which, being of special value to school libraries, carry a comparatively higher price.) Booksellers and publishers pay according to their annual business turnover. Sales to individuals — unless the person maintains a library of some consequence — are separate transactions, with the company assigning a price on the basis of whatever can be learned from the applicant about his use of the requested publication.

Each subscriber submits his own expenditures (or other statistics) at the time of subscribing or at stated intervals. Obviously, it is to his advantage to present a complete and accurate record, for his figures not only determine the charge for his first copy of any book index; they also determine his rate for added copies of these indexes — *for use in the same library* — on a sliding scale supplied to the subscriber on request. (Affiliated libraries within a large system, as in the case of the periodical indexes, pay rates based on their own usage.)

❈ ❈ ❈

Now it is time to hear the critics.*

The service basis policy, as a departure from conventional forms of pricing, has naturally created discussion and dissension. Naturally, too, most of the opposition has been captained by the large libraries, which feel that they are being compelled to pay a relatively high price for the Wilson indexes. The general objections to the policy will be considered first; then the objections pertaining to the periodical indexes; and, finally, the objections related to the book indexes.

Some of the over-all criticism has been extravagant. A number of opponents, for example, have expressed the belief that the whole procedure is absolutely illegal. Yet, actually, no law exists to prevent such a system when it is advanced without concealment and operated without discrimination. Nor does the Robinson-Patman Act, as others have suggested, appear at all relevant. That piece of antitrust legislation is primarily concerned with price-fixing which seeks to destroy competition; and no one has ever seriously accused the Wilson company of being actuated by such a motive in the adoption of the service basis. Two critics, indeed, once wrote to forty-eight state law libraries inquiring if any local statutes outlawed the system. Thirty-two replied — all of

* The following discussion is based upon a series of unpublished reports prepared between 1938 and 1945 by committees and agents of the Association of Research Libraries, an organization of about half a hundred of the largest and most scholarly American libraries, and upon the Wilson company's replies. The reader will find a list of these studies in Appendix III.

them in the negative. That seems to dispose of the question of legality.

But others contend that, if not exactly unlawful, the system is at least unique, implying a rebuke in the use of the term.

The company denies this distinction for its policy. Many national organizations have adopted some sort of graduated scale for membership fees: the Book Publishers Service Bureau, the National Publishers Association, the National Association of Manufacturers, the American Library Association, the Automobile Manufacturers Association, the United States Chamber of Commerce, and countless others. The fees are based on various factors: on volume of business, size of payroll, amount of capital investment, number of production units, or similar criteria; but, regardless of the details, all of these groups use a variation of the service basis. The Wilson company is not being modest but simply accurate in denying the uniqueness of its system.

Other critics maintain that the company's indexing costs are excessive, usually basing the contention on a comparison of the Wilson services with other publications that receive some sort of subsidy. This is hardly fair. If an organization supports an index through membership fees, editorial assistance, or rent-free quarters, the index can often — though not always — be sold at a lower price. Lacking such outside aid, the Wilson indexes must earn enough to cover all their expenses.

That, of course, makes them "commercial enterprises," a term of opprobrium on the lips of some of the more intemperate critics. If it implies that the company has wallowed in profits, the firm's balance sheets discredit the suggestion. Over the years, in fact, profits have been barely sufficient to provide a reasonable return on invested capital and to permit a continuing expansion of service. The company takes pride in that fact, insisting that it constitutes a powerful argument in favor of the service basis as a reasonable method of pricing. It likes also to remind the critics that a ten per cent rebate was distributed to all subscribers for two consecutive war years when government and defense orders raised its profits to abnormal levels.

Another favorite accusation is that the company has permitted popular and profitable publications to carry those of limited appeal. This may have been partially true in the past, though, one should add, it has been an accepted business practice for established ventures to finance new projects in their early years. But the objection is no longer relevant. Rate revisions, some of them drastic, have been adopted recently to ensure that all the publications are self-supporting. Staff members also emphasize that, with increasing experience, the demand for and the price of new services can now be gauged in advance with greater accuracy, so that fewer years of experimentation are required before the publications begin paying their own way.

Still other critics have directed their fire against the company's polling techniques on policy matters, contending that if a library pays on the service basis it should be entitled to vote in the same manner. The company took cognizance of this point of view in 1948 in connection with a poll of *Cumulative Book Index* subscribers on the question of whether, as an economy measure, that publication should be limited to books published in the United States and Canada only or remain "a world list of books in English." Each subscriber was credited with one vote for each dollar of his subscription; but the results were also tabulated, for purposes of comparison, on a straight one-vote-per-subscription basis. Interestingly, the difference between the two methods of tabulation was only 2.2 percentage points: "world listing" won the day with 72.7 per cent of the votes tabulated on the service basis and 70.5 per cent tabulated on the one-vote-per-subscription basis.

Finally, the critics question the Wilson assertion that subscribers paying the minimum prices contribute to editorial and typesetting costs and therefore reduce those costs to all subscribers.

The argument involves a bewildering set of statistics supplied by the company. The figures need not be repeated here. Primarily, the critics object to the company's statement that thirty per cent of every subscription price must be set aside to cover "selling costs." This, they say, is illogical. They agree that varying charges might be valid to cover indexing and composition costs since each customer obtains a different degree of service; but they insist that once a publication has come from the presses, it should not be much more difficult to handle the account of a large subscriber than of a small one. Consequently, each should share the "selling costs" equally. Yet if this is done, they add, it will be revealed that those who pay the minimum price not only fail to make any contribution toward editorial and typesetting expenses, but actually turn out to be a drag upon the big patrons.

The company replies that this argument results from a misunderstanding for which it must assume most of the responsibility.

On releasing its operating data, it made the mistake of stating, without further explanation, that "selling costs" averaged thirty per cent of sales. It should have made abundantly clear that three items are incorporated in "selling costs." The first of these is Promotion — the effort to secure new customers; the second is the Servicing of Subscriptions — postage, billing, bookkeeping, mailing, and the like; and the third is General Administrative Expenses, including each publication's share of salaries that cannot be allocated to any one index and such general costs as taxes, insurance, interest, and depreciation. Only the last of these three items is charged in proportion to the size of the subscription as determined on the service basis. The servicing costs, on the other hand, are paid equally by all subscribers, and the promotion costs are carried exclusively by new customers for a brief period to reimburse the company for its expenditures in attracting their interest.

Thus, the Wilson executives repeat, when these elements of "selling" are properly assigned, the minimum-rate patron not only covers the expenses incurred in the manufacture and distribution of his copy; he makes in addition a small contribution to the fixed costs of indexing and typesetting.

As proof that the larger library does not subsidize the smaller one under the service basis, the company likes to cite the 1949 *Education Index* rate revision, which resulted in substantially lower rates for all subscribers whose periodical holdings had not changed greatly since the last previous checking. This reduction, says the company, was made possible solely by the number of new subscribers added during the intervening years — all of them smaller libraries.

᙮   ᙮   ᙮

The foes of the service basis have four main criticisms of its application to the periodical indexes.

They object, first, to the policy on the *Readers' Guide* of increasing the charge-per-periodical in relation to the number of periodicals received by a library. (It will be recalled that the charge is forty cents each for the first eighty magazines; fifty cents each for the next twenty; and sixty cents for those over a hundred.) The opponents of the plan suggest that this represents a discrimination against the larger libraries.

The company answers that the degree of difficulty in indexing the periodical holdings of the average library increases in direct proportion to the number of magazines in its collection. The library's first acquisitions, in other words, will generally be the popular (and easy to index) magazines; the last will be the scholarly (and hard to index) journals. By the same token, the scholarly periodicals are received by fewer subscribers (among whom the cost of indexing must be divided) than the popular magazines. The modestly graduated scale of the *Readers' Guide* is intended to compensate for these interrelated factors.

The second point of dispute is the method of selecting periodicals for coverage by the indexes.

Some critics contend that every subscriber to an index votes on every nominated magazine regardless of whether or not he will have to pay for its inclusion. That, according to the Wilson staff, is simply not true. The subscriber votes, affirmatively or negatively, *only on the periodicals which he receives*, and he knows at the time that he will have to pay for their inclusion if a majority of the subscribers who take those periodicals approve of their acceptance.

But this is not the end of the complaints about the company's questionnaires. Some of the critics complain that the subscriber does not know the cost of indexing a periodical when he is requested to vote on its inclusion. True; but the company does not know the cost either. That will be determined by the number of libraries receiving the periodical, and the number cannot be known in advance of the poll.

The validity of the whole theory of a price based on use has been denied by still other opponents. The indexes, they argue, may be a guide not only to the subscriber's own collection, but to those available elsewhere and thus subject the larger library to a costly invasion from the outside.

The company replies that the use of periodicals in a larger library by readers who usually patronize a smaller library presupposes a *right* on their part to use the larger institution. It follows that they also have a right to consult the periodical indexes in that institution. The use of indexes in the smaller library, therefore, is a mere convenience, which, incidentally, saves wear on the larger library's copies. The indexes are simply extra keys to the same door, not skeleton keys to open every door. But, in any case, does not borrowing work both ways? The company believes it does, citing as evidence an article in a professional library journal which declares that the larger libraries actually borrow a great deal more than the smaller ones.*

A considerable amount of criticism has also been directed against the editorial aspects of the periodicals indexes. The leaders of the opposition deplore the repeated quotation of titles, the overly frequent cumulations, the excessive bulk resulting from too thorough indexing, the absence of certain important journals, the duplications on the lists of magazines covered by some indexes (although progress has been made toward reducing this in recent years), and the diverse character of such publications as the *Industrial Arts Index.*

Though agreeing that defects exist, the company denies that the situation is quite as alarming as the critics suggest. Some of the duplication, for example, really serves a useful purpose, as shown by the fact that many of the libraries who object to it in principle vote for it in practice in the questionnaires. Moreover, the company reminds the critics that it has constantly consulted librarians in the making of its publications, in the selection of periodicals, in the plan of cumulations, and in the thoroughness of the coverage. It maintains that it has always tried to be guided by the wishes of the subscribers — all of them, big and small, with varying needs. And it promises to be equally responsive in the future, hoping through such cooperation to produce indexes that will most satisfactorily meet the wishes of the largest possible number of libraries.

※　※　※

Two major points are contained in the bill of indictment submitted against the service basis as applied to the book indexes and catalogs.

The first is related to the validity of the library's expenditures as a measure of usefulness. It will be remembered that the present yardstick employed in setting prices for the *Cumulative Book Index* and the other publications in this

* *Library Quarterly,* vol. 2, pp. 113–34 (1932).

category is the average annual sum spent by a library for books *and* periodicals, exclusive of binding, over a three-year period. This, the critics contend, is a faulty gauge. They point out that the *Cumulative Book Index*, like most of the other publications concerned, has nothing whatever to do with periodicals. They insist, moreover, that there is no fixed ratio between book and magazine expenditures: it varies widely between libraries.

The company agrees. It would much prefer to use book expenditures alone as a yardstick; but the present practice has been thrust upon it by the habits of its subscribers. Many libraries, whether large or small, are apparently unable to separate their book and periodical expenditures. Attempts by the company in the past to obtain reports of book expenditures alone have resulted in the utmost confusion, with some libraries reporting correctly and the rest sending an undivided book-and-periodical sum: a situation that produced widespread and serious injustices.

The company has been so concerned with this problem, in fact, that in 1943 it submitted the issue to the Committee on Indexing and Abstracting of the Association of Research Libraries. After due deliberation, this group recommended that the company follow the practice of requesting combined expenditures from all libraries, as the lesser of two evils. Until greater uniformity exists in the bookkeeping practices of the libraries themselves, therefore, the present policy of measuring usefulness (and price) on a yardstick of combined book and periodical expenditures must be continued. Fully aware of its imperfections, the company can only invite suggestions for its improvement, assuring those who disparage it that they will perform a service both to the firm and to the customers by proposing a sound and reasonable alternative.

The second part of the indictment concerns the accuracy with which the rate-scale classifications have been assigned.

When Miles O. Price, librarian of the Law Library at Columbia University, and his wife made an investigation of the service basis in 1938 for the Association of Research Libraries, they found that, using the company's own scale, nearly half of the public libraries and fully three fourths of the university libraries had been incorrectly classified. The company did not always benefit by these errors. On the contrary, more libraries were placed too low than too high on the scale, thus depriving the publisher of considerable revenue. Nonetheless, as one of the investigators observed, this was a "disquieting situation."

But the Prices' report was made more than a decade ago. The company has long since instituted reforms. More personnel has been employed to administer the classifications; the management of the system has been centralized; and the subscribers' accounts have been more frequently overhauled to keep well abreast of existing conditions and of changes in library expenditures. The company firmly believes that if another investigation were conducted today, few, if any, errors in classification would be found.

As this discussion indicates, the service basis system is a complicated instrument which, through mishandling, can easily produce mistakes. It not only demands constant vigilance and intelligence on the part of the Wilson staff; it also requires a high degree of active cooperation from the librarians themselves. If the scheme is to function properly, they must not fail to provide detailed and accurate information or hesitate to complain of seeming injustice. The company, in view of its past record, can certainly be described as a reasonable organization; but it can hardly be expected to understand the problems of a library which does not trouble to explain them.

и и и

That, in brief, is a summary of the criticism leveled against the service basis.

Some of the comments have so impressed the company

that it has altered certain aspects of the policy in conformity with them. Other objections — and the work of preparing a defense against them — have merely confirmed its faith in the basic principles of the system. It remains convinced (1) that the service basis is fair to all libraries; (2) that, under the system, small libraries both pay their own way and make a contribution to editorial and composition costs to the advantage of all; and (3) that the Wilson success story is largely due to the plan.

However, the company is not adverse to investigation by any authorized group. Several such studies have been made, and the investigators have always received generous cooperation. The firm would welcome further exploration of the question — particularly if the interests of the smaller libraries were represented on the committees assigned to the task. This cordiality reflects the company's conviction that it will benefit if libraries have a greater knowledge of the pricing system. Mr. and Mrs. Price made that point in their report: "The compilers believe, as a result of reading dozens of letters from perplexed librarians, that many of them are ignorant of the simplest features of the Wilson service basis. . . . Most of the criticism has been due to this perplexity rather than to dissatisfaction." The company, in response, promised to keep librarians better informed about its methods. The long succession of questionnaires and "open letters" to libraries since that date offers convincing evidence that it has tried to keep its pledge.

This has been an attempt to examine objectively the chief criticisms of the service basis and the company's rejoinders. It can probably be concluded no more helpfully than by quoting an impartial investigator, Professor Stanley F. Teele of the Harvard Graduate School of Business Administration, who submitted the following report on April 2, 1945, at the request of the secretary of the Association of Research Libraries:

"The various indexes and services published by the H. W.

Wilson Company are of great importance to the library world. Although there are necessarily differences in judgment as to the relative importance of particular indexes, there seems to be little disagreement on the importance of the composite product of the Wilson Company.

"With a few relatively minor exceptions, no other individual or organization has ever succeeded in maintaining such servicing over any significant period of years. So far as I am able to determine, the monopoly which is now held by the Wilson Company has been created by repeated exercise of good judgment. The fact that a monopoly has been created may be the cause for some of the considerable amount of irritation displayed by some librarians, since it is a commonly recognized fact that the lack of an alternative induces a sense of frustration and consequently irritation with the cause of the frustration. On the other hand, the fact that the H. W. Wilson Company is the only organization which has succeeded over the years in this highly difficult field gives a strong presumption in favor of the judgment of the Wilson organization as against others.

"The activities of the Wilson Company have not resulted in large profits. Indeed profits have been barely large enough to provide for a moderate return on the capital invested and the expansion in physical assets necessary to provide a growing service.

"With respect to the service basis in general, I can only repeat the approval in principle incorporated in the report of Professors Lewis and Learned and myself made to you in 1940. I have been gratified to note that a number of the specific criticisms of the method of operation incorporated in the original Price Report and emphasized in our report have since either been taken care of or recognized by the Wilson Company to the point where a beginning has been made in improvements.

"Particular attention has been given to one specific question: i.e., do the price schedules result in prices for the smaller libraries which cover the escapable costs? There has been much debate on this question, and I should like to make two or three observations in regard to it. The basic theory is that a certain number of costs will be incurred, regardless of the number of copies of any index which are sold. If the price charged to the smaller libraries covers all the expenses which would not be incurred if sales were not made to them, then any excess may be considered a contribution to the fixed costs incurred, regardless of the number of copies sold, and therefore results in a reduction in price to the larger libraries.

"This question is important, not only from the standpoint of equity among the customers, but even more as a measure of the business judgment of the management. If the price charged to the smaller libraries does not cover the escapable costs, then the more copies sold at this price, the more the company loses.

"In my opinion, the Wilson Company has been weakening its own case in this respect by setting up administrative expenses as if they were escapable costs and allotting them to the copies sold to small libraries and seeking to show a contribution only to editorial costs. In fact, it is much more reasonable to conclude that administrative costs, excluding handling charges, are inescapable, and therefore, that if the minimum prices show a contribution above the truly escapable costs of printing and handling, the pricing is wise from a business judgment standpoint and reasonable from the standpoint of the customers.

"My examination of the figures prepared by the Wilson Company (obviously I did not undertake any new preparation of figures) indicates that in all instances the minimum prices do exceed the truly escapable costs.

"In the last analysis, however, the really important element in pricing in this situation is the judgment of the group concerned. So long as escapable costs are covered by all prices, any management in this situation must use its best judgment, so that the combined sales prices give the best result. From the standpoint of the library world, the key factor is the wholly reasonable profit record resulting from this exercise of judgment.

"My recommendation, therefore, is that all library associations set up or continue regular liaison activities with the Wilson Company to iron out specific details of service and pricing, but that the basic pattern of the Wilson Company's pricing be accepted, and that, in general, the judgment of the management be allowed full scope."

CHAPTER IX

The Elements of Success

The financial risks involved in bibliographic publishing have been constantly stressed throughout this history.

Yet here stands the H. W. Wilson Company . . .

Anyone inclined to question the perils of bibliographic publishing ought to consult a Library of Congress volume which records the various proposals for cooperative cataloging advocated in the last half of the nineteenth century. The list includes almost five hundred plans, nearly all of them described as "feasible," "practical," or "our greatest need." Of these plans, only twenty ever advanced beyond the discussion stage, and fewer still survived the rigorous test of practice.*

Yet here stands the H. W. Wilson Company . . .

The fate of purely commercial ventures, as disclosed in this chronicle, has usually been just as lamentable. They have been born amid great rejoicing, grown anemic on a diet of insufficient support, and died while their helpless founders watched and mourned.

* Torstein Jahr and A. J. Strohm. *Bibliography of Cooperative Cataloging and the Printing of Catalogue Cards . . . (1850–1902).* Washington, Government Printing Office, 1903. 116p. (Reprinted from Report of the Librarian of Congress.)

Yet here stands the H. W. Wilson Company . . .

It has been furnishing prompt, thorough, and accurate indexes and catalogs for more than fifty years — and not just one or two such publications, but literally scores of them. Except in rare instances, it has done so without benefit of subsidies, either directly in the form of grants or indirectly in the form of gratuitous services. It has done so with such remarkable success that stockholders in the firm have received a steady annual income from their investment.

Here stands the H. W. Wilson Company; and many have wondered at the miracle of its survival.

꙾ ꙾ ꙾

Though the company's survival may appear miraculous to those who have counted the casualties littering the bibliographic field, the causes of its success are not really mysterious. Some of them have already been mentioned in this history; others will be pointed out in subsequent pages.

The company, first of all, sought to perform an urgently needed service. Obviously, this was not enough to assure success, for the usefulness of the early enterprises had not sustained them; but their failure did not indicate any indifference on the part of booksellers and librarians. They faltered primarily because of their reliance upon a share-the-work program, which, for a number of reasons, was inefficient: it involved serious delays, prevented uniformity in indexing, imposed restrictions on thoroughness, and precluded economies in production. At the time, however, it seemed to be the only possible course of action. The librarians were willing to share in the editorial labors in proportion to their resources; they were not willing to contribute as generously in money.

This reluctance would probably have destroyed the *Cumulative Book Index* if it had been obliged to be immediately self-sufficient. Fortunately, it was not an orphan. It could depend upon Wilson's bookstore to protect it from the ravages of poverty. The shop did exactly that for fifteen years, during which time the income of the *CBI* was never adequate to cover its expenses.

The service basis for pricing brought an end to the mounting deficits. Regardless of the criticism discussed in the preceding chapter, one fact remains perfectly clear: the company became a modestly prosperous organization soon after the adoption of the policy. Thus it succeeded where the previous attempts had failed: the service basis made possible a centralized force of indexers while providing sufficient monetary support. Financial stability, moreover, permitted the company to improve its existing publications and to launch new ones — both of which developments attracted additional subscribers.

These factors were essential; but personal elements have always been equally important in the company's growth. "Our friends," its twenty-fifth anniversary pamphlet states, "have come all the way with us. They have supported open-mindedly each new venture through the period of experiment. They have offered constructive suggestions and advice. They have heartened us with frequent letters of encouragement and appreciation. They have even had a sympathetic understanding of the company's uncompromising stand always to put first its professional service rather than profit making."

The friends were few in the beginning. The librarians in Minneapolis (particularly Dr. Herbert Putnam, later Librarian of Congress) provided counsel out of their practical experience; the booksellers rallied with subscriptions; the University of Minnesota faculty helped in a multitude of ways. These earlier allies may not have been numerous enough at first to ensure a profit for the new enterprise, but their backing was a vital morale factor in the period of trial.

The character of the company's staff, of course, has been of major importance.

Speaking of his motives in starting the *Cumulative Book*

Index, Wilson once confessed that he might have been infected by a strange disease which, for lack of a better name, he called the Bibliographical Urge. "The germ has not been isolated," he said, "and, consequently, no cure is forthcoming. The malady is almost always financially fatal. The only known relief is a large dose of practicalism to antidote the idealism of the patient. Furthermore, it is contagious and there is always danger that bibliographical idealists who have neither native nor acquired practicalism will communicate the disease to benevolent friends."

Wilson apparently spread the disease among his staff. This may not be a very enlightening explanation of their devotion; but it is difficult to find a more specific one.

What explanation can be offered for Miss Potter's fifty years of faithful service? What kept her at her desk for ten and twelve hours a day? Why did she walk through snowdrifts to reach the office after a midwinter storm? There are many possible answers: an innate sense of duty, respect for the company's founder, delight in the challenge of a responsible job, recognition of its opportunities, pride in accomplishment . . . Probably all these factors were involved; yet, even in combination, they do not seem to be a wholly satisfactory answer.

Miss Potter's own explanation would be much simpler. When someone asked her why she waded through the snow to the office, she replied that she "just had to." Was she being impelled by the Bibliographical Urge? Or was she simply being Miss Potter?

If the explanation implied in that last question can be accepted, it must be observed that Wilson was fantastically lucky (or incredibly shrewd) in his choice of people. For Miss Potter was not alone in her loyalty to the firm. Some of the earliest conscientious workers — Anna L. Guthrie, Edith M. Phelps, and Warren C. Rowell among others — have already been cited; but there were many more who would have been named if space permitted.

Granted that these were exceptional people, however, what welded them together into an effective organization?

Part of the answer no doubt lies in the conditions of work. Ordinarily, in terms of physical plant, these were favorable — though on occasion the constant expansion meant over-crowding for a time. After the construction of the new building near the gateway to the University of Minnesota campus, a company brochure declared: "Generous space, light, and air developed a mentally and physically sturdy staff." It may be so.

The atmosphere of the times cannot be ignored. Veteran employees are fond of recalling their "sense of adventure" during the company's formative years. The phrase referred both to the excitement of pioneering with a new enterprise and to the confidence felt by all Americans when they regarded their nation's future. No one denied that dangers existed even in this tranquil world — particularly, as Anthony Comstock darkly pointed out, for unwary youths; but virtue was a shield against misfortune. The Civil War had become a fast-fading memory, and except for a holiday excursion to Cuba in 1898 and minor battles in remote areas, peace seemed forever secure. Though the western frontier had ceased to be a land of danger and opportunity, there remained the cheerful task of exploring the new frontiers of science and industry. It was late afternoon in an innocent world; but nobody feared the night because the sunset was confused with a new dawn. It was a good time to be alive and working for an even more promising future.

The company also profited from its policy of welcoming women in a period when prejudice barred them from most business firms, and its encouragement of initiative on the part of its workers produced further dividends in loyalty. Its small size was equally significant. Being a highly unified force, the employees may well have been "exalted," as the Wilson house organ proclaimed, by the example of each other's industriousness. The founder, moreover, was able to be thoroughly acquainted with every member of his staff. He could even invite them all, as reported earlier, to a personal conference: "Let each one consider his relation to his job and see me during the month of May, bringing with him plans, suggestions, and troubles."

Naturally, this "family" aspect of the company has not survived into the present. With three hundred and seventy people on the payroll, the president could hardly invite them all to a Christmas party at his house. Other devices, however, have been adopted to promote cordial relations between the management and its employees.

For a time "staff representatives" were elected from each of the major departments, and these people acted as advisers to the Board of Directors, recommending changes in wages, holidays, vacations, and other matters directly affecting the employees. After the passage of the Wagner Labor Relations Act had outlawed such arrangements, the regular unions (the Book and Magazine Guild, the AFL's Book Binders Union, and the "Big Six" typographical unions) set out to organize the company. They met with little success. Believing the firm to be a unique business, the employees felt that no "outside" group was capable of understanding its problems or their needs. Consequently, they formed their own independent and unaffiliated union, the H. W. Wilson Company Employees Association, in 1942. It has been recognized ever since, both by the company and by the federal government, as the exclusive bargaining agent for the staff.

It sounds, of course, suspiciously like a "company" union — meaning a union created and controlled by the company for its own purposes. The leaders of the association are quick to resent any such suggestion, and executives of the firm, especially after a protracted negotiating session, are equally quick to agree. No organization, they insist, could be more zealous in asserting the rights of its members and in seeking additional benefits on their behalf.

The existing contract, signed on July 1, 1949, after weeks

of deliberations, calls for (among other items): the main-
tenance of wage rates for technical personnel at a level com-
parable to that paid in union shops; hospitalization and insurance benefits; a thirty-six-and-a-half-hour work week
with time and a half for overtime; an annual two weeks' vacation with pay and a graduated vacation bonus after the
first six years of service; and nine holidays a year with pay.
Grievances and disputes are settled in three ways: (1) by
conference between the employee and his foreman; (2) by
conference between the employee and the company president, with a representative of the association present if the
employee so desires; and (3) a conference between a committee of the association and the Board of Directors. If no
settlement can be reached in these meetings, an arbitration
board is selected, consisting of two company executives, two
members of the association, and a fifth person chosen by the
four from among those employees who are not eligible for
membership in the association.

This apparatus has seldom been used, for the relationship
between the company and its workers has remained cordial.
The attitude of the directors of the corporation, the knowledge possessed by the association leaders of the company's
unusual position, and the high caliber of the personnel —
these are some of the factors that have contributed to this
friendliness. But there is another: in a large measure, the
employees of the H. W. Wilson Company own the H. W.
Wilson Company.

※　※　※

As recorded in these pages, the firm of Morris & Wilson,
out of which the present corporation grew, was capitalized
originally on two hundred dollars — most of it borrowed
from friends and relatives.

Shortly after the transfer to White Plains in 1913, however, the company was re-incorporated with an authorized capital stock of one hundred and fifty thousand dollars.

Sixty thousand of this was in preferred and the rest in common stock, with the par value of each share set at one hundred dollars.

This stock, incidentally, has rarely paid less than an eight per cent dividend — and never more, save on one occasion to compensate for a reduced dividend in an earlier year.

At the time of the incorporation, only about eight hundred shares were sold. Of this number, Wilson and his wife held almost six hundred. Marion E. Potter, Anna L. Guthrie, Emma L. Teich (then editor of the *Cumulative Book Index*), John B. Doster, and Warren C. Rowell owned about fifty shares each. Three years later the number of employees owning stock had risen to thirty-four. They had invested almost ninety thousand dollars in the company, representing virtually all its outstanding common stock. The balance of the firm's capital, most of it in preferred stock, had been furnished by outside investors. These included professors at the University of Minnesota and a considerable number of librarians in every part of the country.

In the winter of 1918 a staff committee headed by Rowell sent out a letter inviting the employees to invest again in the company. "We wish to emphasize the fact," they wrote, "that no obligation is placed on any one to invest in the stock; but, on the other hand, we feel that cooperation of this sort is of mutual advantage. It encourages thrift by making possible a profitable investment, and one which from small beginnings may develop into something of great importance in time. It is the desire of the management that the employees gradually acquire an increasing interest in the business and that in the course of time no outside capital will be necessary, but that all dividends and surplus profits may be divided among people actively connected with the institution and to whose services its success is due."

A definite step toward this goal was taken in 1934 when a stock distribution plan was put into effect whereby employees were given annual common stock credits in propor-

tion to their earned salary and length of service. After the
adoption of this plan, no further common stock was sold to
outside investors, and the shares in the hands of outsiders
were gradually repurchased by the company or exchanged
for bonds. As a result, more than ninety-nine per cent of the
some three hundred common stockholders (owning about
twenty-four hundred shares) are employees or former employees. A small amount of preferred stock still outstanding
is held chiefly by librarians. Thus the dream of the management expressed in 1918 has largely come true, and the day
cannot be far off when all the company's profits will be divided among the people whose services are responsible for
its prosperity.

Unquestionably, the stock-sharing plan must be added to
the list of factors involved in the firm's astounding success.
That leaves one final element to be considered: the founder
of the company.

×   ×   ×

"I regard him as a genius," wrote a former employee, with
great awe and a little exasperation, of Halsey W. Wilson. "I
have never met a man more anxious to have his life contribute as much as possible to the general welfare. He is
better disciplined to live according to the dictates of his own
conscience and to champion his opinion against all odds, regardless of consequences, than anyone I have ever known."

What manner of man is this who could win such a tribute?

Certainly, in any study of Wilson's career, one is impressed above all with his remarkable patience. The *Cumulative Book Index* lost money for more than a decade; yet
he persisted in publishing it, though the financial drain on
his bookstore often imperiled that prosperous concern. Nearly
all his publications, in fact, have lost substantial sums in
the beginning, and most of them continued to create heavy
deficits for years before becoming solvent. Nonetheless, with
a determination which other men would regard as impru-

dence, he has almost always refused to abandon them. (One of the few exceptions was the *Motion Picture Review Digest*; but it might be noted that, with the appearance of similar services, the need for which the *Digest* had been started was no longer urgent.) He has invested huge amounts of time and cash, moreover, in such ventures as the *United States Catalog*, whose ultimate fate could not be learned for a period of several years.

There was in this persistence none of the born gambler's delight in long shots. Wilson's resolution was based on a firm faith in the eventual triumph of quality. The better mousetrap, in his view, was certain to attract the path-beaters to his door. (That explains, incidentally, the unbaited traps which are scattered throughout the company's offices — including one in bronze on the president's roll-top desk.) Unfortunately, the accuracy of that ancient dictum has never been subjected to a scientific test; but it appears to have been eminently sound in Wilson's case.

Though not always. On his arrival in New York, he lost his way one day and bought a map of the city printed on a single large sheet. Opening it on the street, he was irritated when the wind caught and ripped it. He vowed then to produce a better map and sometime later issued his "Indexed Street Guide and Sectional Map of Manhattan and the Bronx." It was printed in handy sections so the user could consult it even in a hurricane. The vogue of gaudy illustrated maps, however, drove it off the counters. Wilson was mystified. "But," he said, "it's such a *good* map!"

As a guarantee of quality, he has displayed equal patience in devising plans for his publications. The procedures, as he once outlined them, have been as follows: "First, listen to the advice of prospective supporters of a project. If it is important, it will be discussed in librarians' meetings and journals. Then scan the field and study what has been done and why there may have been failures or successes. Consult and secure advice from librarians who may be expected to have an interest in the project. Then the final question: 'If this is a good plan and if we proceed with it, will you plan to subscribe for it?'"

This policy, of course, requires the full cooperation of the librarians. It has succeeded only because they have been willing — out of a desire to promote the development of new professional tools and a respect for the company — to give generously of their time in answering inquiries.

But the policy also demands considerable effort and expense on the part of the company. During the early discussions on the *Union List of Serials*, for example, Wilson spent thousands of dollars and an immeasurable amount of time in designing the style of the book, in preparing and printing sample pages, in checking with librarians on disputed points, and in tabulating the results of his experiments. He had no assurance that these expenditures would ever be recovered. He had nothing to justify his action, indeed, except his faith in the value and feasibility of the project. True, he hoped that his company would be encouraged to launch the list as a result of the promotion. He would then be able, presumably, to regain his initial outlay; but at the time the chances of this seemed extremely remote. Since he had volunteered to perform the work at cost, there was never any question of his acquiring a profit.

That introduces a vital point.

The profit aspect of the business has probably been overly stressed in these pages. It is an understandable mistake of emphasis. After examining the past failures, the temptation to speak at length about Wilson's *profitable* operation is almost irresistible. Yet it is, nonetheless, an error. For profits have always been a secondary consideration with Wilson. He has been anxious, of course, to establish his company on a secure foundation; but that has been a means to an end, not an end in itself. The primary objective has been service.

Now, admittedly, this statement should be greeted with some skepticism. It has become fashionable of late for businessmen to speak virtuously of their work as designed for the public welfare and to scorn their profits as an incidental result accepted by them with great reluctance. But in Wilson's case strong evidence exists to support the contention.

Item: He would never have engaged in bibliographic publishing if his first motive had been profits. Or, if originally ignorant of the economic risks in such ventures, he would have been rapidly educated by his account books at any time during the first fifteen years.

Item: Several of the indexes, as noted above, have consistently lost money in the past; but he kept them alive because he believed them to be highly valuable to a few people. Only at long last did they begin to pay their way.

Item: He has offered on occasion (e.g., the *Union List of Serials*) to publish serviceable books on a nonprofit basis.

Item: Conscious of his unique position of trust, he has always been prepared to open his books for inspection by any authorized person or persons. One of the service basis investigators, it might be added, rebuked the company after examining its accounts for failing to maintain a higher level of profits.

Item: He has been active, at some cost and for no monetary gain, in promoting several projects of usefulness to the whole library profession. Thus, by collecting the opinions of other librarians and by providing expensive samples of the recommended style, he convinced the Library of Congress that it ought to issue a cumulative catalog, in book form, of its printed cards. That campaign resulted in a commendation from Luther H. Evans, Librarian of Congress: "I am certain that without your planning and your urging and your compilation of important information as to the wishes of American libraries we would not have acted as soon as we did. . . . All librarians owe you a great debt of gratitude for your role in this important development. . . ."

Actually, Wilson appears to have little interest in — or at least little use for — money. During the winter he occupies a room in a Bronx hotel at a moderate rental, and since the hotel is only a few blocks from the plant, he has no transportation fares to pay. He eats simple luncheons (usually consisting of soup, pie, and a five-cent package of cookies) in the company's cafeteria. He permits no ostentation in his office — which, strictly speaking, is not an office in the usual sense at all, but an open corner of the fourth floor blocked off by bookcases. However, he does own a handsome colonial house near Yorktown Heights in upper Westchester County, located in the heart of a real estate project which constitutes his chief out-of-office hobby.

Nor does he abandon his habits of economy on business trips. An employee whose expense accounts had been frequently criticized as excessive was once scheduled to accompany Wilson to a library conference. He decided to compare his bill with the one submitted by the president and, on their return, persuaded the cashier to allow him to examine both accounts. Notwithstanding the fact that Wilson had remained one day longer, his expenses were considerably lower. Instead of charging the full price for his meals, he had charged only the difference between the conference meals and those at home. He had also failed to include the price of a berth on the return journey. The employee did not dare to inquire whether he had actually returned in a day coach or had paid for sleeping accommodations out of his own pocket.

If this seems to indicate that Wilson is a parsimonious fellow, the impression must be corrected at once. He is not and never has been a spendthrift. No one who has worked hard all his life, as he has done, would fling money around in a reckless manner. He has apparently no interest whatsoever in "maintaining his social position" if that entails gestures of extravagance. On the other hand, he has always been a generous contributor to causes that he deems worthy of support.

Even if luxuries tempted him, he would have little leisure to enjoy them because his work has absorbed almost all his time. He can seldom remain away from his desk for any extended period. Mrs. Wilson once whisked him off to Florida much against his will; he protested all the way down there, and they were back in ten days. He took a vacation in Europe one summer; but he spent most of his time in foreign archives interviewing librarians about their bibliographic problems and their opinions of the Wilson company's various services.

Any analysis of the company's success must also emphasize Wilson's inventiveness. This history has recorded several incidents in which his ability to devise ingenious procedures has overcome or evaded difficulties that other men might have regarded as impossible barriers. There were, of course, many other similar episodes. He has constantly demonstrated in the field of ideas the same sort of cleverness that Henry Ford exhibited in the mechanical area. It is not surprising, therefore, that Wilson admired the great industrialist: he recognized in him a fellow crusader against those wayward people who cherished a haphazard manner of conducting their affairs.

All these personal details may be considered merely interesting trivia.

Yet they are, in reality, highly significant. The service basis, the income derived from the bookstore, the aid of early friends, the character of the original staff, the stock bonus plan — these and other factors have been important. But there is, at least, an outside chance that the company might have survived even if one of these elements had been missing.

That it could have succeeded without Halsey W. Wilson is inconceivable.

✹ ✹ ✹

The future is another matter, for the company's survival does not depend any more upon a single person.

This is partly due to the quality of the present staff.

Wilson was doubtless interested only in promoting efficiency when he appointed capable men like Howard Haycraft, Charles J. Shaw, Arthur Rigg, and others to important executive posts and filled the editorial chairs and key production jobs with carefully selected personnel either brought up through the company ranks or recruited from the library world. Yet, at the same time, he was providing for the future by building a competent force that could manage the firm at a later period when he would be unable to supervise directly its day-to-day operations.

Through the ownership of stock by employees, moreover, he has guaranteed their continuing loyalty. This does not mean that the employees have an enduring interest in the company only because of the incentive of profit. Most of them would be faithful workers without such a motive. But, unquestionably, the distribution of stock has strengthened their pride in the organization by creating in them a sense of common ownership. The original staff members, in other words, were loyal to their employer; the present staff members are loyal also to their firm.

There is another aspect to be mentioned in regard to the company's future.

Probably no other enterprise relies so heavily upon its customers in the production of its merchandise. The Wilson indexes, in a high degree, are collaborations — not simply among staff members, but also between staff members and subscribers. The strength of the company, therefore, reflects the devotion of librarians to their profession, and it could hardly fail unless the librarians cease to treasure the bibliographic tools which it provides in such abundance. They are not likely to do so if the present quality of the indexes is maintained; and any change for the worse is equally unlikely while the librarians themselves continue to share in the work of producing the indexes.

Thus the company is today much more than the shadow of one man. Without Wilson the firm undoubtedly could not have survived its infancy or its early and middle periods of growth. If it is now so well organized that it could carry on without him — as it someday must — that detracts nothing from Wilson. On the contrary, that fact is a measure of his success: he has built for far more than a lifetime.

CHAPTER X

The Significance

That old autocrat of the breakfast table, Dr. Oliver Wendell Holmes, once addressed a conclave of librarians.

"No extended record of facts," he told them, "grows too old to be useful, provided only that we have a ready and sure way of getting at the particular fact or facts we are in search of. And this leads me to speak of what I conceive to be one of the principal tasks to be performed by the present and the coming generation of scholars, not only in the medical, but in every department of knowledge. I mean the formation of indexes, and more especially of indexes to periodical literature." He lamented that the lack of the "ready and sure way" of locating material condemned the magazines to join "the forlorn brotherhood of 'back numbers.'" Who, he asked, "wants a lock without a key, a ship without a rudder?"

With its publications, the Wilson company provided a whole set of keys; and, as Dr. Holmes realized, those keys enabled men to unlock vast storehouses of information which previously had been barred to them.

❦ ❦ ❦

It is impossible, naturally, to measure the effect of the indexes with any degree of precision. Yet it is certainly reasonable to assume that important changes occurred as a result of them.

The indexes, for example, were responsible in part for altering the character of some of the existing magazines and for creating a demand for new ones. Prior to the twentieth century, the subscribers customarily retained files of their favorite periodicals for reading or rereading in later moments of leisure. They could be fairly certain, in the absence of other distractions, that the future would offer such opportunities; and, meanwhile, they had the necessary storage space in enormous closets, basements, and attics. Then residential architecture, reflecting the growth of urban centers, shifted from spaciousness to compactness, and leisure was all but eliminated by the invention of countless devices for mass entertainment.

At the same time, public and educational libraries emerged from obscurity to positions of importance in the community. Gaining ever wider support, they abandoned their old cramped quarters and moved into imposing structures; with greater space available, they expanded their periodical holdings through gifts and purchases. The public, therefore, began to depend on these institutions for many of the magazines, as well as other reading matter, which the public itself had once owned.

But visiting a library was much more trouble than going downstairs to the cellar. Few people were prepared to make that added effort unless motivated by a compelling desire to do some research within a specialized field. Thus libraries became more interested in stocking reference periodicals than popular journals. However, as space again grew limited, they could not afford to keep even the reference magazines for an indefinite period. There was, indeed, little logic in doing so. Without an index to guide his course, the library patron could not be expected to find his way through a mountainous stack of back numbers to the articles of value to him. But if only the current issues were useful, it was almost

senseless or at least extravagant to subscribe to the magazines in the first place. The librarian, of course, could compile an index of his own holdings; but the high cost of such
an attempt would merely reduce the amount of funds set
aside for book and magazine purchases.

This situation seriously injured the reference periodicals.
They had lost many of their private readers as a result of the
increasing tempo of living; and the lack of an adequate index prevented them from acquiring enough orders from libraries to compensate for the losses. The Wilson indexes,
therefore, gave them a new lease on life, because the libraries, representing in time thousands of subscriptions, took a
renewed interest in them as research sources. It would be
exceedingly strange if that fact did not influence their editorial policies.

But the indexes have had an even greater significance in
terms of their effect upon other fields of learning.

By imposing order on the old chaos of information, they
have been a factor in accelerating the progress of science,
which relies heavily upon the swift exchange of ideas. By
opening a fabulously rich lode of contemporary material,
they have been instrumental in promoting a whole new approach to the writing of modern history. By making research
possible even under the pressure of deadlines, they have
aided in the improvement of all types of journalism. By extending the horizons of knowledge, they have provoked new
experiments in education and agriculture, in art and industry, in law and government.

Undeniably, these statements are largely assumptions,
and there may be little direct evidence to support them. No
scientist has acknowledged his debt to a specific magazine
article located through an index. No historian has proclaimed his reliance upon an index, except by implication in
footnotes and bibliographies. No newspaper reporter or
farmer, no artist or industrial leader, no attorney or political
figure has endorsed the conclusions set forth here. Yet those

conclusions seem reasonable enough to be admitted despite the impossibility of proving them.

Little doubt can exist, however, of the impact of the reference services upon the libraries themselves.

※ ※ ※

The card catalog has been called "the eye of the library," a fanciful image which can be applied with equal accuracy to the Wilson publications.

Obviously, these aids have considerably reduced the librarian's labor in the sheer mechanics of his job: in the selection of books and periodicals, in cataloging and classifying, in advising patrons who seek information on their special interests.

But the indexes are simply tools; and tools are worthless if the owner does not know how to use them. Consequently, the librarian has been obliged to become thoroughly familiar with the indexes. He has to be aware of their special features —the cumulative plan, for instance, which varies slightly with each publication. He must be acquainted with their contents, for the titles are occasionally misleading. (The *Industrial Arts*, one will recall, covers diverse fields like advertising as well as others more readily identified as industrial arts.) He must recognize that not all the indexes are limited to periodicals, that some embrace other pertinent forms of material, such as pamphlets, documents, and books. He must appreciate that the special indexes employ far more specific headings than general ones like the *Readers' Guide*.

The services, moreover, do not relieve him of the task of judgment.

With few exceptions, the Wilson publications are all-inclusive. They list almost every relevant item, making no distinction between the valid and the false, between the important and the trivial. That duty of selection still rests upon the librarian. He has to advise the users of the indexes, and he can do so with wisdom only if he possesses a knowledge of the cited authors, magazines, and publishers. Nor is this always a question of truth and significance. The question of suitability can also be present. An article in *Fortune* may be frivolous in comparison with a learned report in the *Physical Review*. Though the novice researcher may prefer the less technical story in *Fortune*, he might be ignorant of the differences between the two magazines and choose the *Physical Review*. The librarian must be prepared to direct him to the proper sources.

The Wilson company also needs the librarian's help. Many of its catalogs could never have been started without his active cooperation; none of its publications would be satisfactory without his continuing aid. Only he can judge the indexes in terms of daily use. On the basis of his experience, he has an obligation to himself and his profession to suggest desirable changes in methods, propose the inclusion of new material, reply conscientiously to inquiries on policy, and even subject the company to criticism. For genuine criticism, as demonstrated in the discussions of the service basis, can be immensely profitable to all concerned.

The role of counselor and critic has seldom been an easy one. The recent poll on the *Cumulative Book Index* is a case in point. Subscribers were asked whether its scope should be restricted to books published in the United States and Canada, or whether its present world-wide coverage of books in English should be maintained at an increased price. It was an important decision, affecting not merely individual users, but libraries throughout the world. This, as a library school teacher observed, was "a solemn responsibility"; and the subscribers discharged it in that spirit.

Being great time-savers, the Wilson services have helped to liberate the librarian from a bondage to routine chores. Time, however, cannot be deposited in a bank vault; it must be spent. Thus the services pose a new challenge: how can the time be spent to best advantage?

This is certainly not the place for an elaborate study of

library management, even if the writer were qualified to conduct such a study. Yet a few words on the subject cannot be amiss. Librarians and particularly public librarians have seldom been content to be just the custodians of large book collections. "For the library to concern itself only with the loaning of books to registered borrowers," one authority has written, "would be as inadequate as the church concerning itself only with the administration of grace to those who had already been saved."*

An important principle underlies that statement. It is nothing less than the democratic principle of the potential equality of man, with its accompanying faith in man's inherent ability for self-improvement through education. Most public libraries, as well as many private ones, were established to promote that universal instruction; and most of them are still faithfully striving to achieve it.

However, the goal can never be reached unless the librarian has a knowledge not only of his books, but of his readers. He must be fully informed about the community his institution is designed to serve: its skills, religions, nationalities, incomes, birth rate, literacy, and the like. Yet this is not enough. He must also know its reading habits: what it reads, why it reads, where it reads, how it reads. Only then can he select books which will satisfy individual needs without destroying the library's primary function of education.

Even this is not enough.

The librarian must know, in addition, the nonreaders in his area and the causes of their indifference. These will doubtless form a majority of the community and, assuming that democracy depends upon an alert and educated citizenry, will also represent a distinct menace to free government. The librarian will never commit the error of arguing that nonreaders do not want to read. They may wish to read only certain kinds of books; they may be hampered by rural

* James Howard Wellard. *The Public Library Comes of Age.* London, 1940. 204p. Much of this discussion has been based on Wellard's excellent book.

isolation; they may be bewildered by the apparent complexity of the library itself. But they will read if the obstacles are removed. The librarian must set about eliminating those barriers.

Naturally, no library can ever hope to respond to the needs of an entire community. Such an ambitious program would be prohibitively expensive. Nor is it really necessary. Other agencies (newspapers, magazines, rental libraries, bookstores) are available to supply some of the demands.

Thus the librarian, even when guided by the principle of social usefulness, has to discriminate. He must favor those groups whose needs constitute a definite responsibility of a democratic society. The authority quoted above envisions no difficulty in recognizing these needs. "Ignorance, prejudice, maladjustment, and disaffection," he declares, "are faults to correct; intellectual curiosity, tolerance, social well-being, and a community sense are attributes to stimulate."* The terms are broad enough to include the whole community, but at least they suggest some lines of departure in meeting the problem of selection. The librarian has always understood the special needs of such groups as immigrants; he must also realize that other readers can be classified according to their interests — interests shaped by education, age, income, employment, and other factors.

All this converges on the simple statement that the librarian must never forget the role of education which his institution must play in the community. Nor should he allow the community to forget it. This requires an intelligent use of all information outlets, extension work with study groups, exhibits to arouse curiosity, and participation by the librarian in civic affairs. Above all, it demands a constantly expanding knowledge of the community.

Much of this work, of course, has already been done. Much of it, indeed, was begun long before the Wilson indexes and catalogs helped to free the librarian from some of

* *Ibid.*, p. 169.

his routine tasks. But it could never have progressed as far or as fast if those tasks had continued to absorb all the librarian's time and energy.

With some justification, therefore, the Wilson company can claim a small share of the credit for the advances which libraries have made toward their objective of increasing service in the cause of democracy.

Appendixes and Index

SELECTED LIST OF

Wilson Indexes and Services

NOTE. *The titles are arranged in alphabetical order. The dates in parentheses indicate the first year of publication. The editors-in-chief are listed in chronological order. It should be pointed out that the exact editorial relationships were sometimes vague in the early years; but the author believes the names listed are those who held top editorships for significant periods.*

ABRIDGED READERS' GUIDE (1935). See *Readers' Guide to Periodical Literature.*

AGRICULTURAL INDEX (1916). Subject index to some 120 periodicals in Agriculture, Dairy Science, Botany, Forestry, Livestock, Conservation, and other allied fields. Also covers current documents from state experimental stations, U.S. Department of Agriculture, and foreign agricultural agencies; a selected number of agricultural books; occasional pamphlets from nonagricultural sources; and a selected list of college extension bulletins. Published monthly with frequent cumulations; bound annual volumes in September; permanent bound volumes every three years. *Editors*: Neltje Tannehill Shimer; Florence A. Arnold.

ART INDEX (1929). Author-subject index in one alphabet to 118 magazines and museum publications chosen by subscriber votes with the advice of authorities. Illustrations indexed under names of artists. Covers Archeology, Architecture, Graphic Arts, Industrial Design, Landscape Architecture, Painting, Pottery, Sculpture, and related fields. Quarterly issues with cumulated annual volumes replaced by three-year permanent cumulations. *Editors*: Alice M. Dougan; Sarah St. John; Beatrice B. Rakestraw; Margaret Furlong.

BIBLIOGRAPHIC INDEX (1938). Subject index of current bibliographies, including those printed separately as books and pamphlets as well as those appearing as parts of books, pamphlets, and periodical articles. New editions and supplements noted. Issued quarterly, with annual and five-year cumulations. *Editors*: Dorothy Charles; Bea Joseph; Helen Thornton Geer; Virginia Turrell.

BIOGRAPHY INDEX (1946). Covers biographical material in the 1500 periodicals regularly indexed by other Wilson publications; articles in its own special list of legal and medical journals; current books or pamphlets of individual or collective biography printed anywhere in English (including letters, diaries, memoirs, fiction, drama, poetry, pictorial volumes, etc.); prefaces to collected works and anthologies; and obituaries of prominent figures in the *New York Times*. Arranged in two parts: (1) an alphabet of names, and (2) an index by professions. As far as possible, the name entries provide the biographee's full name, vital statistics, nationality, and profession. Published quarterly, with annual and three-year bound cumulations. *Editor*: Bea Joseph.

BOOK REVIEW DIGEST (1905). "Devoted to the valuation of current literature," the *Digest* annually lists about 4000 books by author, with price, publisher, and other bibliographic details; quotations from a subscriber-selected group of eighty periodicals; and descriptive notes. A cumulated title-and-subject index appears in a separate alphabet. Published monthly except in July, with semiannual and annual cumulations. Every fifth annual cumulation contains a cumulated subject-and-title index of books covered during the five-year period. *Editors*: Clara E. Fanning and Justina Leavitt Wilson; Margaret Jackson; Mary K. Reely; Marion A. Knight; Mertice M. James and Dorothy Brown.

CATALOG OF REPRINTS IN SERIES (1940). An annual list of reprints available in all important adult and juvenile series. Two sections: (1) an alphabetical section by author and title, and (2) a series section, with price and description, arranged under the publishers' names. *Editor*: Robert M. Orton.

CHILDREN'S CATALOG (1909). See *Standard Catalog Series*.

CUMULATIVE BOOK INDEX (1898). A world list of current books in the English language by author, title, subjects, editor, translator, illustrator, or series — all in one alphabet. Price, publisher, binding, paging, size, date of publication, Library of Congress card order number, and availability of Wilson printed catalog card are noted in the main entries. A directory of publishers is appended. Monthly supplements, cumulating frequently, with an annual bound volume except in those years when a larger cumulation (including the last year of the period) is issued. *Editors*: Marion E. Potter; Emma L. Teich; Agnes Van Valkenburgh; Eleanor E. Hawkins; Mary Burnham; Regina Goldman.

CURRENT BIOGRAPHY (1940). "Who's News and Why": a magazine supplying reliable and up-to-date sketches with photographic portraits; obituary notices of distinguished personages; references to other published material; and pronunciation of difficult names. Published monthly, with a cumulated index to previous issues and a bound yearbook. *Editors*: Maxine Block; Anna Rothe.

EDUCATION INDEX (1929). Covers completely more than 120 leading educational periodicals in the U.S., Canada, and foreign countries. Listings are by author and subject in one alphabet. Divided into six sections: (1) notes on new publications and pending educational meetings; (2) list of indexed periodicals and yearbooks; (3) key to abbreviations; (4) directory of publishers; (5) checklist of professional books, educational association reports, and relevant documents from government agencies; and (6) the main author-and-subject index. Published monthly, with frequent cumulations except in the summer months; annual and three-year cumulations. *Editors*: Lily Belle Voegelein; Isabel L. Towner; Dorothy Ross Carpenter.

EDUCATIONAL FILM GUIDE (1936). See *Standard Catalog Series*.

ESSAY AND GENERAL LITERATURE INDEX (1931). See *Standard Catalog Series*.

FICTION CATALOG (1908). See *Standard Catalog Series*.

FILMSTRIP GUIDE (1948). See *Standard Catalog Series*.

INDEX TO LEGAL PERIODICALS (1908). An author-and-subject index to more than 100 legal magazines and to bar association reports. Compiled by the American Association of Law Libraries; published and distributed on a commission basis by the Wilson company. Issued monthly with annual and three-year cumulations.

INDUSTRIAL ARTS INDEX (1913). Monthly cumulative subject index of more than 200 periodicals covering Industry, Finance, Public Administration, Advertising, Science (Chemistry, Physics, Geology), Insurance, Aviation, Engineering, Economics, Printing, and other related fields. Bound annual volumes, complete in one alphabet, printed in December. *Editor*: Marion E. Potter.

INTERNATIONAL INDEX TO PERIODICALS (1907). Originally issued as a *Readers' Guide* supplement, this index became a separate publication six years later. It indexes by author and subject a selected list of some 175 magazines devoted to pure science and the humanities: history, international affairs, political science, sociology, psychology, philosophy, and some twenty other specialties. Only English language periodicals were indexed during World War II, but the foreign language coverage was restored in 1948. Published on a quarterly schedule, with annual cumulations; permanent cumulated volumes printed every three years. *Editors*: Anna Lorraine Guthrie; Mary Esther Robbins; Elizabeth J. Sherwood; Alice F. Muench; Dorothy Charles.

LIBRARY LITERATURE (1936). An author-and-subject index and digest to current books, pamphlets, and periodicals relating to the library profession. Publication was suspended for 1943–45, but material for that period will eventually be included in a permanent three-year volume. *Editors*: Marian Shaw; Dorothy Ethlyn Cole.

READERS' GUIDE TO PERIODICAL LITERATURE (1901). An author-and-subject index in one alphabet to 117 magazines selected by subscriber votes. Published semimonthly from September through June and monthly in July and August, with frequent cumulations. An annual volume appears in March and a permanent cumulated volume every two years. Designed for smaller libraries, the *Abridged Readers' Guide to Periodical Literature* (1935) covers only 35 of the magazines surveyed in the full edition. Published monthly except during June and July, with frequent cumulations; annual number issued in May. Like the unabridged edition, it has a permanent cumulation at the end of a two-year period. *Editors*: Anna Lorraine Guthrie; Marion A. Knight; Elizabeth Sherwood; Alice M. Dougan; Sarita Robinson.

REFERENCE SHELF (1922). Each number — six numbers constituting a volume — contains selected articles and addresses, with a full bibliography, on a question of current interest. Published irregularly. *Editors*: Edith M. Phelps; John Jamieson.

STANDARD CATALOG SERIES (1909). *Editors and associate editors*: Marion E. Potter; Minnie Earl Sears; Dorothy E. Cook; Isabel S. Monro;

Dorothy Herbert West. *Sub-editors:* Siri Andrews; Corinne Bacon; Zaidee Brown; Agnes Cowing; Anne T. Eaton; Ruth Giles; Katharine M. Holden; Frederic A. Krahn; Eva Rahbek-Smith; Beatrice B. Rakestraw; Marian Shaw.

Standard Catalog for Public Libraries (1934). Covering nonfiction books, this catalog includes a basic volume listing some 12,000 titles, with annual supplements containing about 600 to 800 titles. After eight years the supplements and basic volume are combined to provide a new basic volume. The catalog can be used as a guide in purchasing books; as a reference tool in locating specific books, in seeking material on a specific subject, or in preparing library catalog cards; and as a training guide for courses in good book selection. It is divided into two parts. The first section, arranged according to the Dewey Decimal Classification system, offers a complete listing of each book — including author, title, publisher, copyright date, retail price, additional subject headings, and a brief description prepared by the Wilson staff or extracted from reviews. Books recommended for first purchase by small libraries are marked with a star; those especially recommended are double-starred. The second section consists of a straight dictionary index by author, title, and subject and by analytical entries referring to parts of books included in the catalog. For details on methods of selecting the books, see pp. 69–70.

Standard Catalog for High School Libraries (1926). Covering both fiction and nonfiction, this catalog has a basic volume (4500 titles) with semiannual supplements (200 to 300 titles). The basic volume and the supplements are combined every five years to make a new basic volume. The editorial arrangement is similar to the public library catalog, except that the two main sections are reversed: the first indexes the books by author, title, subject, and analytical entries in one alphabet; the second lists them according to the Dewey system. The latest edition (1947) includes a list of 600 titles especially selected for Catholic schools.

Children's Catalog (1909). List of new fiction and nonfiction of interest to children. The series includes a basic volume and annual supplements, a revised basic volume appearing every five years. It is similar in editorial arrangement to the two preceding catalogs, except that the annotations are included in the alphabetical, not the classified, section. It also presents a selected list of books by school grades.

Educational Film Guide (1936). Full subject-and-title catalog of current 16 mm. films suitable for educational purposes. Schedule of publication: nine monthly issues, with three quarterly cumulations and a bound annual cumulation in September. The cumulations include a selection of 100 to 150 titles from monthly numbers — described, evaluated, graded, and arranged according to the Dewey Decimal Classification system.

Essay and General Literature Index (1931). Analyzes books of essays in all fields and other important reference works of a composite nature. Arranged in a single alphabet that includes all author and subject entries and such title entries as appear necessary. A list of analyzed books is printed in a back section. Issued semiannually, the midyear number in July and the annual cumulated volume in February. Every two or three years a further cumulation is prepared, and every seven years a permanent cumulated volume appears.

Fiction Catalog (1908). A list of 5500 works of fiction in English, arranged by subject, author, and title (plus annotations) in a single alphabet. Includes a basic volume and annual supplements which are combined every ten years to form a new basic volume.

Filmstrip Guide (1948). This is a subject-and-title catalog of still pictures. It is similar in arrangement to *Educational Film Guide* but omits selective lists in its cumulations.

Wilson Printed Catalog Cards (1938). This service catalogs newly published books which, on the basis of library reports, reviews, and other material, seem likely to appear in *Standard Catalog* supplements. Two different sets of cards — the number in each varying with the nature of the book but averaging four or five — are available: (1) WITH the Dewey numbers and subject headings at the top, or (2) WITHOUT this printed information. Sets for some 1800 titles are printed annually. Librarians can purchase all the sets on a subscription basis or order individual sets.

UNION LIST OF SERIALS (1927). Published with the cooperation of an Advisory Committee of the American Library Association, the *Union List* contains some 120,000 serial titles and indicates the holdings of about 650 libraries. The second edition of more than 3000 pages appeared in 1943. The first supplement, covering 1941–43 acquisitions and changes, with some 1944 material, was published in 1945.

UNITED STATES CATALOG (1899). The latest edition (1928) lists 190,000 books published in the United States and in print January 1, 1928, arranged by title and subject in 3175 three-column pages. The catalog is kept up to date by current and cumulated numbers of the *Cumulative Book Index. Editors*: see *Cumulative Book Index.*

UNIVERSITY DEBATERS' ANNUAL (1915). Each volume includes nine or ten collegiate debates of the year accompanied by selected briefs and bibliographies. A list of the contents is furnished on request. *Editors*: E. Clyde Mabie; Edith M. Phelps; Ruth Ulman.

VERTICAL FILE SERVICE (1932). An annotated subject index, in dictionary form, of available pamphlets, booklets, leaflets, and mimeographed items. It serves as a buying guide and a reference tool. Published monthly (about 400 titles) except in August, with an annual cumulation (about 4500 titles). *Editors*: Anna Rothe; Phyllis Crawford; Florence D. Phin.

WILSON LIBRARY BULLETIN (1914). See pp. 80–81. *Editors*: Edith M. Phelps; Stanley J. Kunitz; Howard Haycraft; Marie D. Loizeaux.

WILSON PRINTED CATALOG CARDS (1938). See *Standard Catalog Series.*

CHRONOLOGICAL LIST OF THE COMPANY'S
General Publications

NOTE. *These are original issues only; reprints and revisions are not included except in the instance of books taken over from other publishers, in which case the earliest Wilson edition is listed.*

1900
Manual of elementary practical physics for high schools. By Julius Hortvet.

1901
System of qualitative chemical analysis, by Staedeler, Kolbe, and Abeljanz. Authorized and revised translation by George B. Frankforter.

1902
Index to the *Forum*, vols. i to xxxii. Compiled by Anna Lorraine Guthrie.
Manual of physical measurements. By Anthony Zeleny and Henry Anton Erikson.
Postelsia; yearbook of the Minnesota seaside station.

1903
Education in Minnesota. By David L. Kiehle.
Geography and geology of Minnesota. By Christopher Webber Hall.
Philosophy of Hobbes in extracts and notes collated from his writings. Edited by Frederick James Eugene Woodbridge.

1904
Chemical urinalysis. By Hubert C. Carel.
Constitutions and other select documents illustrative of the history of France, 1789–1901. By Frank Maloy Anderson.
Course in elementary mechanical drawing. By William A. Pike.
Culture and anarchy, and selections from the essays of Matthew Arnold. With a prefatory note by Charles F. McClumpha.

Directory of booksellers, librarians, publishers and stationers in the United States.
Elements of differentiation and integration. By John F. Downey.
Foundry practice. By James Murray Tate and Melvin Oscar Stone.
Guide to the Dalles of the St. Croix. By Charles Peter Berkey.
Inorganic chemical syllabus. By Hubert C. Carel.
Introduction to the summation of the differences of a function. By Benjamin F. Groat.
Laboratory directions in general zoology. By Charles P. Sigerfoos.
Laboratory guide in entomology. By Oscar W. Oestlund.
Manual of anatomy. By Charles A. Erdman.
Minnesota stories.
Old English prose texts. By Frederick Klaeber.
Optimistic equation and other optimism. By E. Bird.
Outline and references for American history, with special reference to constitutional development. By Willis Mason West.
Pictorial and historical souvenir of the University of Minnesota.
Prose types. Edited by Ada Comstock and Edward Stanford.
Simpler elements of analytical geometry. By George N. Bauer.
Syllabus of general geology. By Christopher Webber Hall.

1905

St. John's fire; a drame in four acts, by Hermann Sudermann. Translated from the German by Grace E. Polk.

1906

Cruise and capture of the *Alabama.* By Albert M. Goodrich.
Deutsche gedichte. Compiled by Carl Schlenker and Hans Juergensen.
Directory of booksellers in the United States and Canada.
Laboratory notes and directions in general plant morphology (algae, fungi, lichens) . . . By Josephine Elizabeth Tilden.
Selected articles on the enlargement of the United States navy. Compiled by Clara Elizabeth Fanning. (Debaters' handbook series.)
Studies in constitutional history. By James O. Pierce.

1907

Directory of libraries in the United States and Canada.
Quantitative metallurgical analysis. Edited by Charles Frederick Sidener.
Swedish grammar and reader. By J. S. Carlson.

1909

Selected articles on capital punishment. Compiled by Clara Elizabeth Fanning. (Debaters' handbook series.)
Selected articles on the commission plan of municipal government. Compiled by Edwin Clyde Robbins. (Debaters' handbook series.)
Selected articles on the election of United States senators. Compiled by Clara Elizabeth Fanning. (Debaters' handbook series.)
Selected articles on the initiative and referendum. Compiled by Edith May Phelps. (Debaters' handbook series.)
University addresses by William Watts Folwell.

1910

Addresses, educational and patriotic, by Cyrus Northrop.

Government insurance of bank deposits.

Handbook of United States public documents. By Elfrida Everhart.

Outlines of entomology. By Oscar W. Oestlund.

Picture collection. By John Cotton Dana. (Modern American library economy series.)

Selected articles on a central bank of the United States. Compiled by Edwin Clyde Robbins. (Debaters' handbook series.)

Selected articles on direct primaries. Compiled by Clara Elizabeth Fanning. (Debaters' handbook series.)

Selected articles on the income tax, with special reference to graduation and exemption. Compiled by Edith May Phelps. (Debaters' handbook series.)

Selected articles on woman suffrage. Compiled by Edith May Phelps. (Debaters' handbook series.)

1911

Debating societies. By Rollo LaVerne Lyman.

Human cry. Poems by Richard Warner Borst.

Selected articles on child labor. Compiled by Edna Dean Bullock. (Debaters' handbook series.)

Selected articles on federal control of interstate corporations. Compiled by Edith May Phelps. (Debaters' handbook series.)

Selected articles on municipal ownership. Compiled by Edna Dean Bullock and Joy Elmer Morgan. (Debaters' handbook series.)

Selected articles on parcels post. Compiled by Edith May Phelps. (Debaters' handbook series.)

Selected articles on the compulsory arbitration of industrial disputes. Compiled by Lamar Taney Beman. (Debaters' handbook series.)

Selected articles on the employment of women. Compiled by Edna Dean Bullock. (Debaters' handbook series.)

Selected articles on the open versus closed shop. Compiled by Edwin Clyde Robbins. (Debaters' handbook series.)

Selected articles on the recall. Compiled by Julia Emily Johnsen. (Abridged debaters' handbook series.)

Syllabus for Economics I, interpolated with expository, critical, and interpretative matter. By Raymond Vincent Phelan.

1912

High school debate book. By Edwin Clyde Robbins.

Library work, cumulated 1905–1911; a bibliography and digest of library literature. Edited by Anna Lorraine Guthrie.

Selected articles on compulsory insurance. Compiled by Edna Dean Bullock. (Debaters' handbook series.)

Selected articles on free trade and protection. Compiled by Joy Elmer Morgan. (Debaters' handbook series.)

Selected articles on government ownership of railroads. Compiled by Edith May Phelps. (Debaters' handbook series.)

Selected articles on government ownership of the telegraph. Compiled by Edith May Phelps. (Abridged debaters' handbook series.)

Selected articles on the fortification of the Panama canal. Compiled by Clara Elizabeth Fanning. (Abridged debaters' handbook series.)

South America, past and present.

1913

Children's books for Sunday school libraries. Compiled by Clara L. Herbert.
Selected articles on minimum wage. Compiled by Mary Katharine Reely. (Abridged debaters' handbook series.)
Selected articles on Panama canal tolls. Compiled by Edith May Phelps. (Abridged debaters' handbook series.)
Selected articles on reciprocity. Compiled by Edwin Clyde Robbins. (Debaters' handbook series.)
Selected articles on ship subsidy. Compiled by Caroline A. Clifford. (Abridged debaters' handbook series.)
Selected articles on the conservation of natural resources. Compiled by Clara Elizabeth Fanning. (Debaters' handbook series.)
Selected articles on the six-year presidential term. Compiled by Estelle E. Painter. (Abridged debaters' handbook series.)
Selected articles on trade unions. Compiled by Edna Dean Bullock. (Debaters' handbook series.)

1914

American book publishers, 1914.
Best books on the war. Compiled by Corinne Bacon.
Handbook of the European war. Edited by Stanley Solomon Sheip and Alfred Bingham. (Handbook series.)
Library jokes and jottings. By Henry T. Coutts.
Literacy test for immigrants, 1913–1914. (Iowa State university debates.)
Minimum wage, a debate. (Chicago university debates.)
Popular books for boys and girls. Compiled by Carrie E. Scott.
Rocky mountain flowers. By Frederic Edward Clements and Edith Schwartz Clements.
Selected articles on government ownership of telegraph and telephone. Compiled by Katharine Berry Judson. (Debaters' handbook series.)
Selected articles on world peace, including international arbitration and disarmament. Compiled by Mary Katharine Reely. (Debaters' handbook series.)
Toaster's handbook; jokes, stories, and quotations. Compiled by Clara Elizabeth Fanning and Harold Workman Williams.

1915

Active citizenship. Edited by Charles Davidson. (Study outline series.)
Agricultural credit. Compiled by Edna Dean Bullock.
Baby's rights, from birth to third year. Compiled by the Newark (N.J.) free public library.
Contemporary English literature, a study outline. Edited by Arthur Beatty. (Study outline series.)
Debaters' manual. Compiled by Edith May Phelps. (Debaters' handbook series.)
Description of federal public documents. By Lawrence C. Wroth.
Educational test for immigrants. By Edwin Du Bois Schurter and E. I. Francis.
Eighty tales of valor and romance for boys and girls. Compiled by the children's department of the Cleveland public library.
England and Scotland, history and travel, a study outline. Edited by Clara Elizabeth Fanning. (Study outline series.)

Flowers of mountain and plain. By Edith Schwartz Clements.

Home economics, a study outline. Prepared by the home economics division, agricultural extension department, Purdue university. (Study outline series.)

Index to short stories. Compiled by Ina Ten Eyck Firkins.

Italian art, general survey, a study outline. Prepared by the Wisconsin library commission. (Study outline series.)

Library adventures of Bob and Elizabeth. By Marie Louise Prevost.

Lists of stories and programs for story hours. Edited by Effie L. Power.

Mexico, a study outline. By L. E. Stearns. (Study outline series.)

Municipal civics, a study outline. Edited by Anna Lorraine Guthrie. (Study outline series.)

Present day industries in the United States, a study outline. Prepared by the study club department of the Wisconsin library commission. (Study outline series.)

Selected articles on immigration. Compiled by Mary Katharine Reely. (Debaters' handbook series.)

Selected articles on military training. Compiled by Corinne Bacon. (Abridged debaters' handbook series.)

Selected articles on mothers' pensions. Compiled by Edna Dean Bullock. (Debaters' handbook series.)

Selected articles on national defense (vol. 1). Compiled by Corinne Bacon. (Debaters' handbook series.)

Selected articles on prohibition of the liquor traffic. Compiled by Lamar Taney Beman. (Debaters' handbook series.)

Selected articles on single tax. Compiled by Edna Dean Bullock. (Debaters' handbook series.)

Selected articles on the Monroe doctrine. Compiled by Edith May Phelps. (Debaters' handbook series.)

Selected articles on the recall, including the recall of judges and judicial decisions. Compiled by Edith May Phelps. (Debaters' handbook series.)

Selected articles on unemployment. Compiled by Julia Emily Johnsen. (Debaters' handbook series.)

Short ballot. Compiled by Edna Dean Bullock. (Handbook series.)

Slav peoples, a study outline. By Gregory Yarros. (Study outline series.)

Socialism. Compiled by Edwin Clyde Robbins. (Handbook series.)

South America; topical outlines for twenty club meetings, with bibliography. Edited by Corinne Bacon. (Study outline series.)

Studies in modern plays, a study outline. By Hannah Amelia Davidson. (Study outline series.)

Subject index to about five hundred societies which issue publications relating to social questions. Compiled by the Newark (N.J.) free public library.

United States since the Civil war, a study outline. Edited by Clara Elizabeth Fanning. (Study outline series.)

University debaters' annual; constructive and rebuttal speeches delivered in debates of American colleges and universities during the college year 1914–1915. Edited by Edward Charles Mabie.

What makes a novel immoral? By Corinne Bacon.

What shall we read now? Compiled by the Pratt institute free library and the free public library of East Orange.

1916

Aids in high school teaching. By John Cotton Dana and Blanche Gardner. (Modern American library economy series.)

Care of pamphlets and clippings in libraries. By Philena A. Dickey. (Library problems series.)

City beautiful, a study of town planning and municipal art. Edited by Kate Louise Roberts. (Study outline series.)

Daily newspapers in the United States. By Callie Wieder. (Practical bibliographies.)

Early American literature, a study outline. Edited by Anna Lorraine Guthrie. (Study outline series.)

Libraries; addresses and essays by John Cotton Dana.

Library aids for teachers and school librarians. By Esther M. Davis and Agnes Cowing.

Library bookbinding. By Arthur L. Bailey.

Masters of American journalism. By Julia Carson Stockett. (Practical bibliographies.)

Selected articles on national defense (vol. 2). Compiled by Corinne Bacon. (Debaters' handbook series.)

Selected articles on non-resistance. Compiled by Mary Prescott Parsons. (Abridged debaters' handbook series.)

Some great American newspaper editors. Compiled by Margaret Ely. (Practical bibliographies.)

Things I like to do for boys and girls. Compiled by Lillian Sutherland.

University debaters' annual; constructive and rebuttal speeches delivered in debates of American colleges and universities during the college year 1915–1916. Edited by Edward Charles Mabie.

Woman suffrage, a study outline. Edited by Justina Leavitt Wilson. (Study outline series.)

1917

Americanization. Compiled and edited by Winthrop Talbot. (Handbook series.)

Book of Carnegie libraries. By Theodore Wesley Koch.

Books for Christmas for the children. Compiled by Corinne Bacon.

Checklist of indexed periodicals. Compiled by Alvan Witcombe Clark.

Children's library, a dynamic factor in education. By Sophy H. Powell.

Contemporary American literature, a study outline. Edited by Anna Lorraine Guthrie. (Study outline series.)

Library work with children. Compiled by Alice Isabel Hazeltine. (Classics of American librarianship.)

List of references on the history of the reformation in Germany. Compiled by George Linn Kieffer. (Practical bibliographies.)

Poisonous gas in warfare: application, prevention, defense and medical treatment. By Henry Ernest Haferkorn and Felix Neumann.

Prison reform. Compiled by Corinne Bacon. (Handbook series.)

Public regulation of the rate of wages. By Rinehart J. Swenson.

Questions of the hour: social, economic, industrial. Edited by Justina Leavitt Wilson. (Study outline series.)

Russia, history and travel, a study outline of eighteen programs and a bibliography. Edited by Clara Elizabeth Fanning. (Study outline series.)

Russian literature, a study outline. Edited by Anna Lorraine Guthrie. (Study outline series.)

Selected articles on military training in schools and colleges, including military camps (vol. 1). Compiled by Agnes Van Valkenburgh. (Debaters' handbook series.)

Selected articles on minimum wage. Compiled by Mary Katharine Reely. (Debaters' handbook series.)

1600 business books. Compiled by Sarah B. Ball.

Some of the best dramas. By Francis Keese Wynkoop Drury.

Subject headings for the information file, with notes on setting up a file of ephemera. Compiled by Lois M. Wenman and Miriam Ogden Ball.

University debaters' annual; constructive and rebuttal speeches delivered in debates of American colleges and universities during the college year 1916–1917. Edited by Edith M. Phelps.

Vocational education. Compiled by Emily Robison. (Handbook series.)

Vocational education and guidance of youth, an outline for study. Edited by Emily Robison. (Study outline series.)

1918

Canons of classification applied to "the subject," "the expansive," "the decimal," and "the library of congress" classification; a study in bibliography, classification, methods. By William C. Berwick Sayers. (Coptic series for librarians.)

Country life and rural problems, a study outline. By Mary Katharine Reely. (Study outline series.)

List of references on birth control. Compiled by Theodore Schroeder. (Practical bibliographies.)

Office methods. Compiled by Blanche Baird Shelp. (Practical bibliographies.)

Selected articles on a League of nations. Compiled by Edith May Phelps. (Handbook series.)

Selected articles on Russia; history, description and politics. Compiled by Clara Elizabeth Fanning. (Handbook series.)

Selected articles on the city manager plan of government. Compiled by Edward Charles Mabie. (Debaters' handbook series.)

University debaters' annual; constructive and rebuttal speeches delivered in debates of American colleges and universities during the college year 1917–1918. Edited by Edith M. Phelps.

1919

American art. Edited by Anna Lorraine Guthrie. (Study outline series.)

Choosing a play; suggestions and bibliography for the director of amateur dramatics. By Gertrude E. Johnson.

Contemporary drama. Edited by Arthur Beatty. (Study outline series.)

Daily bread; [three] one-act plays. By Mary Katharine Reely.

New poetry, a study outline. Edited by Mary Prescott Parsons. (Study outline series.)

School library management. By Martha Wilson.

Selected articles on athletics. Compiled by Julia Emily Johnsen. (Abridged debaters' handbook series.)

Selected articles on employment management. Compiled and edited by Daniel Bloomfield. (Handbook series.)

Selected articles on military training in schools and colleges, including military camps (vol. 2). Compiled by Agnes Van Valkenburgh. (Debaters' handbook series.)

Travel in the United States. Edited by Clara Elizabeth Fanning. (Study outline series.)

University debaters' annual; constructive and rebuttal speeches delivered in debates of American colleges and universities during the college year 1918–1919. Edited by Edith M. Phelps.

1920

Employees' magazines for factories, offices, and business organizations. By Peter Francis O'Shea.

Index to St. Nicholas, vols. 1–45, 1873–1918. Compiled by Anna Lorraine Guthrie.

Librarian's open shelf; essays on various subjects. By Arthur Elmore Bostwick.

Library and society. Edited by Arthur Elmore Bostwick. (Classics of American librarianship.)

Library essays; papers related to the work of public libraries. By Arthur Elmore Bostwick.

Plays for children, a selected list. Compiled by Kate Oglebay.

Selected articles on national defense (vol. 3). Compiled by Julia Emily Johnsen. (Debaters' handbook series.)

Selected articles on problems of labor. Compiled by Daniel Bloomfield. (Handbook series.)

Selected articles on restriction of immigration. Compiled by Edith May Phelps. (Abridged debaters' handbook series.)

Selected articles on the American merchant marine. Compiled by Edith May Phelps. (Debaters' handbook series.)

Standard practice in personnel work. By Eugene Jackson Benge.

2400 business books, and guide to business literature. By Linda Huckel Morley and Adelaide Cecilia Kight, under the direction of John Cotton Dana.

University debaters' annual; constructive and rebuttal speeches delivered in debates of American colleges and universities during the college year 1919–1920. Edited by Edith M. Phelps.

1921

Catalog of literature for advisers of young women and girls. Compiled by Anna Eloise Pierce.

Directions for the librarian of a small library. By Zaidee Brown and revised by Anna G. Hall.

Henrik Ibsen; a bibliography of criticism and biography with an index to characters. Compiled by Ina Ten Eyck Firkins. (Practical bibliographies.)

Indexing, a handbook of instruction. By George Edward Brown. (Coptic series.)

Library advertising. By Walter Alwyn Briscoe. (Coptic series.)

Modern social movements; descriptive summaries and bibliographies. By Savel Zimand.

On buying and using print, practical suggestions from a librarian to the business man. By John Cotton Dana.

Open shop, a debate. By Andrew Furuseth and Walter Gordon Merritt.

Plays for amateurs, a selected list. Prepared by the New York drama league.

Selected articles on current problems in taxation. Compiled by Lamar Taney Beman. (Handbook series.)

Selected articles on disarmament. Compiled by Mary Katharine Reely. (Handbook series.)

Selected articles on immigration. Compiled by Edith May Phelps. (Handbook series.)

Selected articles on independence for the Philippines. Compiled by Julia Emily Johnsen. (Abridged debaters' handbook series.)

Selected articles on the closed shop. Compiled by Lamar Taney Beman. (Handbook series.)

Selected articles on the Negro problem. Compiled by Julia Emily Johnsen. (Handbook series.)

Selected articles on the study of Latin and Greek. Compiled by Lamar Taney Beman. (Handbook series.)

Style book, a compilation of rules governing the style used in setting the publications of the H. W. Wilson Company.

University debaters' annual; constructive and rebuttal speeches delivered in debates of American colleges and universities during the college year 1920–1921. Edited by Edith M. Phelps.

1922

Aerial photography. By Henry Ernest Haferkorn.

Cancellation of the allied debt. Compiled by Julia Emily Johnsen. (Reference shelf.)

Cataloging rules with explanations and illustrations. By Dorcas Fellows.

China and Japan; a study outline. Compiled by Julia Emily Johnsen. (Reference shelf.)

Christmas in poetry. Compiled by the Carnegie library school association.

Four hour day in coal; a study of the relation between the engineering of the organization of work and the discontent among the workers in the coal mines. By Hugh Archbald.

Free speech bibliography, including every discovered attitude toward the problem covering every method of transmitting ideas and of abridging their promulgation upon every subject matter. By Theodore Schroeder.

Guide to the use of libraries; a manual for college and university students. By Margaret Hutchins, Alice Sarah Johnson, and Margaret Stuart Williams.

An introduction to library classification, theoretical, historical, and practical, and a short course in practical classification, with readings, questions and examination papers. By William Charles Berwick Sayers.

Kansas court of industrial relations. Compiled by Julia Emily Johnsen. (Reference shelf.)

More toasts; jokes, stories and quotations. Compiled by Marion Dix Mosher.

Practical psychology for business executives. Compiled by Lionel Danforth Edie. (Modern executive's library.)

St. Lawrence river ship canal. Compiled by Julia Emily Johnsen. (Reference shelf.)

Selected articles on social insurance. Compiled by Julia Emily Johnsen. (Handbook series.)

University debaters' annual; constructive and rebuttal speeches delivered in debates of American colleges and universities during the college year 1921–1922. Edited by Edith M. Phelps.

1923

Books on the Pacific northwest for small libraries. Compiled by Eleanor Ruth Rockwood.

Classified guide to 1700 annuals, directories, calendars and year books. Compiled by Harry George Turner Cannons.

County library systems; their history, organization and administration. By Duncan Gray.

County rural libraries, their policy and organization. By Robert Duncan Macleod.

Enforcement of the decisions of the Railway labor board. Compiled by Lamar Taney Beman. (Reference shelf.)

Financial incentives for employees and executives. Compiled and edited by Daniel Bloomfield. (Modern executive's library.)

Illustrative material for high school literature. By Jane Anderson Hilson and Katherine Eleanor Wheeling.

Ku Klux klan. Compiled by Julia Emily Johnsen. (Reference shelf.)

List of subject headings for small libraries. Edited by Minnie Earl Sears.

Permanent court of international justice. Compiled by Julia Emily Johnsen. (Reference shelf.)

Problems in personnel management. Compiled and edited by Daniel Bloomfield. (Modern executive's library.)

Quarter century of cumulative bibliography; retrospect and prospect.

Questions of the hour. Compiled by Justina Leavitt Wilson. (Reference shelf.)

Repeal of the prohibition amendment. By Ransom H. Gillett and John Haynes Holmes. (Reference shelf.)

Screw threads. By Henry Ernest Haferkorn.

Selected articles on current problems in municipal government. Compiled by Lamar Taney Beman. (Handbook series.)

Ship subsidies. Compiled by Lamar Taney Beman. (Reference shelf.)

State censorship of motion pictures. Compiled by J. R. Rutland. (Reference shelf.)

Thanksgiving in poetry. Compiled by the Carnegie library school association.

University debaters' annual; constructive and rebuttal speeches delivered in debates of American colleges and universities during the college year 1922–1923. Edited by Edith M. Phelps and Julia E. Johnsen.

War with Mexico, 1846–1848. By Henry Ernest Haferkorn.

1924

Anthracite question. By Hilmar Stephen Raushenbush.

Collection of decisions presenting principles of wage settlement. Edited by Herbert Feis.

Development of common law in industry. By Herbert Feis. (Modern executive's library.)

French occupation of the Ruhr. Bates college versus Oxford union society of Oxford college, City Hall, Lewiston, Maine, September 27, 1923. (Reference shelf.)

Independence for the Philippines. Compiled by Julia Emily Johnsen. (Reference shelf.)

The library and its organization. Edited by Gertrude Martha Gilbert Drury. (Classics of American librarianship.)

The modern executive. Compiled and edited by Daniel Bloomfield. (Modern executive's library.)

One hundred plays for out-door theatres; a selected list. Compiled by Sara Trainor Floyd.

Power of Congress to nullify supreme court decisions. Compiled by Dormin J. Ettrude. (Reference shelf.)

Publicity for public libraries. By Gilbert Oakley Ward.

Reference list of bibliographies: chemistry, chemical technology, and chemical engineering since 1900. Compiled by Julian Arell Sohon.

Restriction of immigration. Compiled by Edith May Phelps. (Reference shelf.)

Selected articles on prohibition, modification of the Volstead law. Compiled by Lamar Taney Beman. (Handbook series.)

Soldiers' bonus. Compiled by Julia Emily Johnsen. (Reference shelf.)

The strike for union. By Heber Blankenhorn.

Superpower. Compiled by Lamar Taney Beman. (Reference shelf.)

University debaters' annual; constructive and rebuttal speeches delivered in debates of American colleges and universities during the college year 1923–1924. Edited by Edith M. Phelps.

1925

Academic freedom. Compiled by Julia Emily Johnsen. (Reference shelf.)

Bookman's reading and tools. By Halsey William Wilson.

Fundamentalism versus modernism. Compiled by Eldred Cornelius Vanderlaan. (Handbook series.)

Japanese exclusion. Compiled by Julia Emily Johnsen. (Reference shelf.)

Labor party for the United States. Compiled by James Goodwin Hodgson. (Reference shelf.)

The library and its contents. Edited by Harriet Price Sawyer. (Classics of American librarianship.)

A list of books for girls. Compiled by Effie Louise Power.

Professional education for librarianship. By Tai Tse-Chien.

Proportional representation. Compiled by Lamar Taney Beman. (Reference shelf.)

Recognition of Soviet Russia. Compiled by James Goodwin Hodgson. (Reference shelf.)

Selected articles on birth control. Compiled by Julia Emily Johnsen. (Handbook series.)

Selected articles on capital punishment. Compiled by Lamar Taney Beman. (Handbook series.)

Selected articles on child labor. Compiled by Julia Emily Johnsen. (Handbook series.)

Selected articles on marriage and divorce. Compiled by Julia Emily Johnsen. (Handbook series.)

Selected articles on school library experience. Compiled by Martha Wilson. (Librarians' round table.)

Selection and care of sound investments. By Arthur Hobart Herschel.

Single six-year term for President. Compiled by Edith May Phelps. (Reference shelf.)

Slavonic nations of yesterday and today; select readings and references on Russia, Poland, Czechoslovakia, Yugoslavia and Bulgaria. Edited by Milivoy S. Stanoyevich. (Debaters' handbook series.)

Tax-exempt securities. Compiled by Lamar Taney Beman. (Reference shelf.)

University debaters' annual; constructive and rebuttal speeches delivered in debates of American colleges and universities during the college year 1924–1925. Edited by Edith M. Phelps.

1926

Abolishment of the electoral college. Compiled by Lamar Taney Beman. (Reference shelf.)

Anthony Trollope: a bibliography. Prepared by Mary Leslie Irwin.

Arbor day in poetry. Compiled by the Carnegie library school association.

Child labor. Compiled by Julia Emily Johnsen. (Reference shelf.)

Direct primary. Compiled by Lamar Taney Beman. (Reference shelf.)

Discriminating duties and the American merchant marine. By Lloyd W. Maxwell.

Easter in poetry. Compiled by the Carnegie library school association.

Election versus appointment of judges. Compiled by Lamar Taney Beman. (Reference shelf.)

Exit Miss Lizzie Cox, a bibliotherapeutic tragedy in one act. By Anna Morris Boyd.

Federal department of education. Compiled by Julia Emily Johnsen. (Reference shelf.)

Government regulation of the coal industry; supplementary to handbook "Government ownership of coal mines." Compiled by Julia Emily Johnsen. (Reference shelf.)

Metric system. Compiled by Julia Emily Johnsen. (Reference shelf.)

Military training compulsory in schools and colleges. Compiled by Lamar Taney Beman. (Reference shelf.)

Mother's day in poetry. Compiled by the Carnegie library school association.

Novels too good to miss. Compiled by Francis Keese Wynkoop Drury.

Outlawing the pistol. Compiled by Lamar Taney Beman. (Reference shelf.)

Periodicals of international importance: a selection of 600 useful in libraries everywhere. Compiled by Edith May Phelps.

Selected articles on criminal justice. Compiled by James Patrick Kirby. (Handbook series.)

Selected articles on evolution. Compiled by Edith May Phelps. (Handbook series.)

Selected articles on states rights. Compiled by Lamar Taney Beman. (Handbook series.)

Selected articles on unemployment insurance. Edited by Allen Bennett Forsberg. (Handbook series.)

Selected articles on war — cause and cure. Compiled by Julia Emily Johnsen. (Handbook series.)

Spanish literature in English translation; a bibliographical syllabus. By Angel Flores.

Special legislation for women. Compiled by Julia Emily Johnsen. (Reference shelf.)

Story terrace. By Frances Elizabeth Atchinson.

University debaters' annual; constructive and rebuttal speeches delivered in debates of American colleges and universities during the college year 1925–1926. Edited by Edith M. Phelps.

1927

Agriculture and the tariff. Compiled by Julia Emily Johnsen. (Reference shelf.)

Business books: 1920–1926. Compiled by Linda Huckel Morley and Adelaide Cecilia Kight, under the direction of John Cotton Dana.

Civil liberty. Compiled by Edith May Phelps. (Reference shelf.)

Farm relief. Compiled by Lamar Taney Beman. (Reference shelf.)

Find it yourself, a brief course in the use of books and libraries. Edited by Elizabeth Scripture and Margaret R. Greer.

Independence for the Philippines. Compiled by Eleanor Ball. (Reference shelf.)

Index to plays, 1800–1926. Compiled by Ina Ten Eyck Firkins.

The library and the Joneses. By Clara Martin Baker.

The library without the walls. Edited by Laura M. Janzow. (Classics of American librarianship.)

Memorial day in poetry. Compiled by the Carnegie library school association.

Our ancient liberties; the story of the origin and meaning of civil and religious liberty in the United States. By Leon Whipple.

Prohibition, modification of the Volstead law. Compiled by Lamar Taney Beman. (Reference shelf.)

Questions of the hour. Compiled by Julia Emily Johnsen. (Reference shelf.)

Religious teaching in the public schools. Compiled by Lamar Taney Beman. (Reference shelf.)

Selected articles on a federal department of education. Compiled by Julia Emily Johnsen. (Handbook series.)

Selected articles on commercial arbitration. Compiled and edited by Daniel Bloomfield. (Handbook series.)

Selected articles on old age pensions. Compiled by Lamar Taney Beman. (Handbook series.)

Union list of serials in libraries of the United States and Canada. Edited by Winifred Gregory, with an advisory committee appointed by the American library association.

University debaters' annual; constructive and rebuttal speeches delivered in debates of American colleges and universities during the college year 1926–1927. Edited by Edith M. Phelps.

Washington and Lincoln in poetry. Compiled by the Carnegie library school association.

1928

Bibliography of the Negro in Africa and America. Compiled by Monroe Nathan Work.

Book revue; a pageant for children's book week. By Maude Stewart Beagle.

Cabinet form of government. Compiled by Julia Emily Johnsen. (Reference shelf.)

Federal and state control of water power. Compiled by Julia Emily Johnsen. (Reference shelf.)

Five day week. Compiled by Lamar Taney Beman. (Reference shelf.)

Flood control. Compiled by Lamar Taney Beman. (Reference shelf.)

Flower families and ancestors. By Frederic Edward Clements and Edith Schwartz Clements.

Flowers of coast and sierra, with thirty-two plates in color. By Edith Schwartz Clements.

Jury system. Compiled by Julia Emily Johnsen. (Reference shelf.)

Library key; an aid in using books and libraries, with an appendix, Short cuts to information. By Zaidee Mabel Brown.

Plant succession and indicators. By Frederic Edward Clements.

Selected articles on China yesterday and today. Compiled by Julia Emily Johnsen. (Handbook series.)

Selected articles on interallied debts and revision of the debt settlements. Compiled by James Thayer Gerould and Laura Shearer Turnbull. (Handbook series.)

Selected articles on interlibrary loans. Compiled by James Adelbert McMillen. (Librarians' round table.)

Selected articles on intervention in Latin America. Compiled by Lamar Taney Beman. (Handbook series.)

Selected articles on national defense. Compiled by Julia Emily Johnsen. (Handbook series.)

Selective cataloging: Catalogers' round table, American library association, July 3, 1924. Edited by Henry Bartlett Van Hoesen. (Librarians' round table.)

University debaters' annual; constructive and rebuttal speeches delivered in debates of American colleges and universities during the college year 1927–1928. Edited by Edith M. Phelps.

1929

Baumes law. Compiled by Julia Emily Johnsen. (Reference shelf.)

Bibliography on the teaching of the social studies. Selected and arranged by Edgar C. Bye.

Financing of state highways. Compiled by Julia Emily Johnsen. (Reference shelf.)

Government fund for unemployment. Compiled by Helen Marie Muller. (Reference shelf.)

Guide to material on crime and criminal justice; a classified and annotated union catalog of books, monographs, pamphlets. Edited by Augustus Frederick Kuhlman.

Installment buying. Compiled by Helen Marie Muller. (Reference shelf.)

Interscholastic athletics. Compiled by Julia Emily Johnsen. (Reference shelf.)

Lantern lists. 8 booklets compiled by Zaidee Brown: Books of adventure, Cheerful books, From past to present in America, Little guide to English novelists, Romance from foreign lands, Some good historical novels, Tales of the sea, To read aloud.

The library and its workers. Edited by Jessie Sargent McNiece. (Classics of American librarianship.)

The library within the walls. Edited by Katharine Twining Moody. (Classics of American librarianship.)

Manual of cataloging and classification for small school and public libraries. By Margaret Fullerton Johnson.

Organization of knowledge and the system of the sciences. By Henry Evelyn Bliss.

Our holidays in poetry. Compiled by Mildred Priscilla Harrington, Josephine H. Thomas, and the Carnegie library school association.

Selected articles on compulsory automobile insurance; liability and compensation for personal injury. Edited by Edison Louis Bowers. (Handbook series.)

Selected articles on the pact of Paris; officially the general pact for the renunciation of war. Compiled by James Thayer Gerould. (Handbook series.)

Thirteen-month calendar. Compiled by Julia Emily Johnsen. (Reference shelf.)

University debaters' annual; constructive and rebuttal speeches delivered in debates of American colleges and universities during the college year 1928–1929. Edited by Edith M. Phelps.

1930

Book shop; a book review presenting a progressive series of books from kindergarten to grade eight. By Rosa Lila Sasloe.

Conscription of wealth in time of war. Compiled by Julia Emily Johnsen. (Reference shelf.)

County libraries. Compiled by Julia Emily Johnsen. (Reference shelf.)

County manager government. Compiled by Helen Marie Muller. (Reference shelf.)

Debate coaching, a handbook for teachers and coaches. By Corroll Pollock Lahman. (Handbook series.)

Disarmament. Compiled by Julia Emily Johnsen. (Reference shelf.)

Free trade. Compiled by Julia Emily Johnsen. (Reference shelf.)

Illustrative material for junior and senior high-school literature. By Katherine Eleanor Wheeling and Jane Anderson Hilson.

Locating books for interlibrary loan, with a bibliography of printed aids which show location of books in American libraries. By Constance Mabel Winchell.

Mother Goose for modern goslings. By Anne Wakely Jackson.

Selected articles on chain, group, and branch banking. Compiled by Virgil Willit. (Handbook series.)

Selected articles on law enforcement. Compiled by Julia Emily Johnsen. (Handbook series.)

Selected articles on trends in retail distribution, including a brief on chain stores. Compiled and edited by David Bloomfield. (Handbook series.)

Socialization of medicine. Compiled by Edith May Phelps. (Reference shelf.)

A source book for vocational guidance; choice selections and references for counselors, home-room teachers, and others concerned with the guidance of youth. By Edna Elizabeth Watson.

Teaching the use of books and libraries; a manual for teachers and librarians. By May Ingles and Anna McCague.

University debaters' annual; constructive and rebuttal speeches delivered in debates of American colleges and universities during the college year 1929–1930. Edited by Edith M. Phelps.

1931

Best books of our time, 1901–1925. Compiled by Asa Don Dickinson.

Capitalism on trial. Compiled by Julia Emily Johnsen. (Reference shelf.)

Censorship and the public library, with other papers by George Franklin Bowerman.

Chain stores. Compiled by Daniel Bloomfield. (Reference shelf.)

Child training and parent education; references to materials in recent books. By Lucile Reiner Stebbing.

Compulsory unemployment insurance. Compiled by Ezra Christian Buehler. (Reference shelf.)

County unit of school administration. Compiled by William George Carr. (Reference shelf.)

Genera of fungi. By Frederic Edward Clements and Cornelius Lott Shear.

Living authors. Edited by Stanley Jasspon Kunitz. (Authors series.)

Lobbying in Congress. Compiled by Helen Marie Muller. (Reference shelf.)

One thousand best books, the household guide to a lifetime's reading and clue to the literary labyrinth. Compiled by Asa Don Dickinson.

Outstanding novels of the twentieth century. Compiled by Ruth Melamed.

Planning for economic stability. Compiled by James Goodwin Hodgson. (Reference shelf.)

Plays for junior and senior high school. Compiled by Marjorie Seligman and Louise Michelbacher Frankenstein.

Practical bibliography making with problems and examples. By Martha Conner.

Selected articles on censorship of the theater and moving pictures. Compiled by Lamar Taney Beman. (Handbook series.)

Selected articles on recognition of Soviet Russia. Compiled by Ezra Christian Buehler, Bertram Wayburn Maxwell, and George Raymond Roy Pflaum. (Handbook series.)

Stability of employment. Compiled by Julia Emily Johnsen. (Reference shelf.)

Trends in university education. Compiled by James Goodwin Hodgson. (Reference shelf.)

Union list of periodicals in special libraries of the New York metropolitan district. Edited by Ruth Savord and Pearl M. Keefer.

Union list of serials in libraries of the United States and Canada: supplement, July 1925–June 1931. Edited by Gabrielle E. Malikoff, with an advisory committee appointed by the American library association.

United States government publications as sources of information for libraries. By Anne Morris Boyd.

University debaters' annual; constructive and rebuttal speeches delivered in debates of American colleges and universities during the college year 1930–1931. Edited by Edith M. Phelps.

Water transportation: Harbors, ports and port terminals; a bibliography, guide and union catalog. By Mirl Edison Pellett.

The world court. Compiled by Helen Marie Muller. (Reference shelf.)

1932

Alice in wonderland, a dramatic version. Arranged by Clara Childs Puckette.

Cancellation of international war debts. Compiled by James Goodwin Hodgson. (Reference shelf.)

Concordance to the poems of Ralph Waldo Emerson. By George Shelton Hubbell.

Debate index. Edited by Edith May Phelps. (Reference shelf.)

Education by radio. Compiled by Helen Marie Muller. (Reference shelf.)

English Shakesperian criticism in the eighteenth century. By Herbert Spencer Robinson.

Federal regulation of banking, with guaranty of deposits. Compiled by James Goodwin Hodgson. (Reference shelf.)

List of subject headings for information file. Compiled by Lois M. Wenman. (Modern American library economy series.)

Nineteenth century novels. Compiled by Ruth Melamed.

Polish literature in English translation; a bibliography with a list of books about Poland and the Poles. Compiled by Eleanor Edwards Ledbetter.

Selected articles on government ownership of coal mines. Compiled by Julia Emily Johnsen. (Handbook series.)

State and local tax revision. Compiled by Ezra Christian Buehler. (Reference shelf.)

State and local tax revision; analytical survey. Compiled by Ezra Christian Buehler. (Reference shelf.)

Still more toasts; jokes, stories and quotations. Compiled by Helen Marie Muller.

Union list of serial publications of foreign governments, 1815–1931. Edited by Winifred Gregory for the American council of learned societies, American library association, and National research council.

University debaters' annual; constructive and rebuttal speeches delivered in debates of American colleges and universities during the college year 1931–1932. Edited by Edith M. Phelps.

The victory of peace. By Florence Eckert.

1933

American vs. British system of radio control. Compiled by Ezra Christian Buehler. (Reference shelf.)

Authors today and yesterday. Edited by Stanley Jasspon Kunitz, Howard Haycraft, and Wilbur Crane Hadden. (Authors series.)

Bibliography of time study engineering or time study, motion study, wage incentives and fatigue in industry. Compiled by the research committee of the Buffalo chapter of the Society of industrial engineers.

Biography in collections, suitable for junior and senior high schools. By Hannah Logasa.

Chinese-Japanese war. Compiled by Julia Emily Johnsen. (Reference shelf.)

Dramatic bibliography; an annotated list of books on the history and criticism of the drama and stage and on the allied arts of the theatre. Compiled by Blanch Merritt Baker.

Economic nationalism. Compiled by James Goodwin Hodgson. (Reference shelf.)

Famous first facts; a record of first happenings, discoveries and inventions in the United States. By Joseph Nathan Kane.

Federal aid to education. Compiled by Julia Emily Johnsen. (Reference shelf.)

Federal regulation of motor transport. Compiled by Helen Marie Muller. (Reference shelf.)

Increasing the President's power. Compiled by Julia Emily Johnsen. (Reference shelf.)

The library and its home. Edited by Gertrude Martha Gilbert Drury. (Classics of American librarianship.)

The library as a vocation. Edited by Harriet Price Sawyer. (Classics of American librarianship.)

Magazines, the untapped reservoirs of new ideas; a guide to the use of magazines in the library.

Make your own job; opportunities in unusual vocations. By Violet Ryder.

Massachusetts, state name, flag, seal, song, bird, flower, and other symbols. By George Earlie Shankle.

Minnesota, state name, flag, seal, song, bird, flower, and other symbols. By George Earlie Shankle.

Organization of knowledge in libraries, and the subject-approach to books. By Henry Evelyn Bliss.

Practical suggestions for the beginner in subject heading work. By Minnie Earl Sears.

Selected articles on capitalism and its alternatives. Compiled by Julia Emily Johnsen. (Handbook series.)

Stabilization of money. Compiled by James Goodwin Hodgson. (Reference shelf.)

Student library assistant; a workbook bibliography and manual of suggestions. By Wilma Bennett.

Union list of serials in libraries of the United States and Canada: supplement, July 1931–December 1932. Edited by Gabrielle E. Malikoff, with an advisory committee appointed by the American library association.

University debaters' annual; constructive and rebuttal speeches delivered in debates of American colleges and universities during the college year 1932–1933. Edited by Edith M. Phelps.

Virginia, state name, flag, seal, song, bird, flower, and other symbols. By George Earlie Shankle.

Washington, state name, flag, seal, song, bird, flower, and other symbols. By George Earlie Shankle.

Who's who in library service. Edited by Charles Clarence Williamson and Alice Louise Jewett.

1934

Author index to a guide to material on crime and criminal justice. By Augustus Frederick Kuhlman.

Bibliography of crime and criminal justice, 1927–1931. Compiled by Dorothy Campbell Culver.

Contest debating; a textbook for beginners. By Harrison Boyd Summers. (Reference shelf.)

Federal aid for the equalization of educational opportunity. Compiled by Helen Marie Muller. (Reference shelf.)

Government ownership of public utilities. Compiled by James Goodwin Hodgson. (Reference shelf.)

Industrial standardization; its principles and application. By John Gaillard.

International traffic in arms and munitions. Compiled by Julia Emily Johnsen. (Reference shelf.)

Junior book of authors, an introduction to the lives of writers and illustrators for younger readers, from Lewis Carroll and Louisa Alcott to the present day. Edited by Stanley Jasspon Kunitz and Howard Haycraft. (Authors series.)

Library manual; a study-work manual of lessons on the use of books and libraries. By Marie Antoinette Toser.

Occupations and vocational guidance. Compiled by Wilma Bennett.

Sales taxes, general and retail. Compiled by Daniel Bloomfield. (Reference shelf.)

Selected articles on the problem of liquor control. Compiled by Julia Emily Johnsen. (Handbook series.)

Some aspects of cooperative cataloging. By Ernest Cushing Richardson.

State names, flags, seals, songs, birds, flowers, and other symbols. By George Earlie Shankle.

Teacher's key for library manual. By Marie Antoinette Toser.

Twelve inch shelf, a pocket library of economics. By John W. Herring and Ethel C. Phillips.

University debaters' annual; constructive and rebuttal speeches delivered in debates of American colleges and universities during the college year 1933–1934. Edited by Edith M. Phelps.

Wall Street, asset or liability? Compiled by James Goodwin Hodgson. (Reference shelf.)

Who reads what? By Charles H. Compton.

1935

Background readings for American history. Compiled by Jean Carolyn Roos. (Reading for background.)

Books about Spain. Compiled by Mabel Williams.

Census of medieval and renaissance manuscripts in the United States and Canada (vol. 1). By Seymour de Ricci.

Collective bargaining. Compiled by Julia Emily Johnsen. (Reference shelf.)

Democratic collectivism. Compiled by Helen Marie Muller. (Reference shelf.)

Doctoral dissertations accepted by American universities. No. 1, 1933–1934. Edited by D. B. Gilchrist.

Doctoral dissertations accepted by American universities. No. 2, 1934–1935. Edited by D. B. Gilchrist.

Limitation of power of supreme court to declare acts of Congress unconstitutional. Compiled by Julia Emily Johnsen. (Reference shelf.)

Lotteries. Compiled by Helen Marie Muller. (Reference shelf.)

Materials for a life of Jacopo da Varagine. By Ernest Cushing Richardson.

More first facts; a record of first happenings, discoveries and inventions in the United States. By Joseph Nathan Kane.

Old age pensions. Compiled by Julia Emily Johnsen. (Reference shelf.)

Readings for French, Latin, German; a bibliography of materials for atmosphere and background for pupils in foreign language classes. Edited by Alice Rebecca Brooks. (Reading for background.)

Reconstruction in Hungary, 1924–1935; bibliography of magazine articles. Compiled by Meda Lynn.

Socialization of medicine. Compiled by Julia Emily Johnsen. (Reference shelf.)

Speech index; an index of 64 collections of world famous orations and speeches for various occasions. Compiled by Roberta Briggs Sutton.

A system of bibliographic classification. By Henry Evelyn Bliss.

University debaters' annual; constructive and rebuttal speeches delivered in debates of American colleges and universities during the college year 1934–1935. Edited by Edith M. Phelps.

What shall we read next? A program of reading sequences. Compiled by Jean Carolyn Roos. (Reading for background.)

1936

American literary annuals and gift books, 1825–1865. By Ralph Thompson.

Bibliographies and summaries in education to July 1935. Compiled by Walter S. Monroe and Louis Shores.

Bibliographies of twelve Victorian authors. Compiled by Theodore George Ehrsam and Robert H. Deily, under the direction of Robert M. Smith.

Bibliography of dancing. Compiled by Paul David Magriel.

British authors of the nineteenth century. Edited by Stanley Jasspon Kunitz and Howard Haycraft. (Authors series.)

Composers of today; a comprehensive biographical and critical guide to modern composers of all nations. Compiled and edited by David Ewen.

Consumers' cooperatives. Compiled by Julia Emily Johnsen. (Reference shelf.)

Crisis in the electric utilities. By Jasper Vanderbilt Garland and Charles F. Phillips. (Reference shelf.)

Doctoral dissertations accepted by American universities. No. 3, 1935–1936. Edited by D. B. Gilchrist.

Freedom of speech. Compiled by Julia Emily Johnsen. (Reference shelf.)

Government ownership of electric utilities. Compiled by Julia Emily Johnsen. (Reference shelf.)

Guides to study material for teachers in junior and senior high schools, junior colleges, adult education classes. By Mary Evelyn Townsend and Alice Gertrude Steward. (Social science service series.)

Index to holiday plays for schools; a guide to plays for the observance of all the holidays and special days and weeks celebrated in the schools. Compiled by Hilah Coddington Paulmier.

Index to vocations. Compiled by Willodeen Price and Zelma E. Ticen.

Learning to use the library in the junior high school; a manual consisting of individualized lessons to be given in English classes. By Florence Damon Cleary.

Literary characters drawn from life. By Earle Francis Walbridge.

Natural history index-guide. Compiled by Brent Altsheler.

Neutrality policy of the United States. Compiled by Julia Emily Johnsen. (Reference shelf.)

Official publications relating to American state constitutional conventions. Prepared by the document section of the University of Chicago libraries.

Selected articles on minimum wages and maximum hours. Compiled and edited by Egbert Ray Nichols. (Handbook series.)

So this is the catalog! Compiled by the junior members round table of the American library association.

Specimens of reading lists. By Francis Keese Wynkoop.

Three pageants. By Josephine Wilhelm Wickser.

Unemployment relief documents; guide to the official publications and releases of F.E.R.A. and the 48 state relief agencies. By Jerome K. Wilcox.

Unicameral legislatures. Compiled by Harrison Boyd Summers. (Reference shelf.)

University debaters' annual; constructive and rebuttal speeches delivered in debates of American colleges and universities during the college year 1935–1936. Edited by Edith M. Phelps and Julia E. Johnsen.

1937

American book of days. By George William Douglas.

American newspapers, 1821–1936, a union list of files available in the United States and Canada. Edited by Winifred Gregory under the auspices of the Bibliographical society of America.

American nicknames: their origin and significance. By George Earlie Shankle.

Arbitration and the National labor relations board. Compiled by Egbert Ray Nichols and James W. Logan. (Reference shelf.)

Audio-visual aids for teachers in junior and senior high schools, junior colleges, adult education classes. By Mary Evelyn Townsend and Alice Gertrude Stewart.

Best books of the decade, 1926-1935. Compiled by Asa Don Dickinson.

Children's books from foreign languages. Compiled by Ruth A. Hill and Elsa de Bondeli.

Classification of books; an inquiry into its usefulness to, the reader. By Grace Osgood Kelley.

Classification of business literature. By the Graduate school of business administration, Harvard university.

Composers of yesterday; a biographical and critical guide to the most important composers of the past. Compiled and edited by David Ewen.

Contributions to the art of music in America by the music industries of Boston, 1640–1936. By Christine Merrick Ayars.

Doctoral dissertations accepted by American universities. No. 4, 1936–1937. Edited by D. B. Gilchrist.

Hollywood's movie commandments; a handbook for motion picture writers and reviewers. By Olga Johanna Martin.

Industrial versus craft unionism. Compiled by Julia Emily Johnsen. (Reference shelf.)

Modern group discussion, public and private. By Lyman Spicer Judson. (Reference shelf.)

Motion pictures in education. Compiled by Edgar Dale, Fannie Wyche Dunn, Charles Francis Hoban, and Etta Schneider.

Publicity primer: An a b c of "telling all" about the public library. By Marie Duvernoy Loizeaux.

Reorganization of the supreme court. Compiled by Julia Emily Johnsen. (Reference shelf.)

Science books for the elementary school. Edited by Ruth Budd. (Reading for background.)

Time savers, the periodical indexes. Compiled by the junior members round table of the American library association.

Unicameralism in practice, the Nebraska legislative system. Compiled by Harrison Boyd Summers. (Reference shelf.)

University debaters' annual; constructive and rebuttal speeches delivered in debates of American colleges and universities during the college year 1936–1937. Edited by Edith M. Phelps and Julia E. Johnsen.

1938

American authors, 1600–1900; a biographical dictionary of American literature. Edited by Stanley Jasspon Kunitz and Howard Haycraft. (Authors series.)

Anglo-American agreement. By Harrison Boyd Summers. (Reference shelf.)

Background readings in music. Compiled by Ruth Estelle Bradley. (Reading for background.)

Bibliographies in American history. By Henry Putney Beers.

Book and library plays for elementary and high school use (vol. 1). Edited by Edith May Phelps.

Chinese-Japanese war, 1937. Compiled by Julia Emily Johnson. (Reference shelf.)

Communication through the ages; a bibliography of materials for atmosphere and background for pupils in junior high school. Compiled by Edith M. Stoddard and edited by Helen S. Carpenter. (Reading for background.)

Dictatorships versus democracies, 1938. Compiled by Harrison Boyd Summers and Robert Edward Summers. (Reference shelf.)

Discussion methods explained and illustrated. By Jasper Vanderbilt Garland. (Reference shelf.)

Doctoral dissertations accepted by American universities. No. 5, 1937–1938. Edited by D. B. Gilchrist.

Educational work in museums of the United States; development, methods and trends. By Grace Fisher Ramsey.

Government spending and economic recovery. Edited by Charles Franklin Phillips and Jasper Vanderbilt Garland. (Contemporary social problems discussion series.)

International congresses and conferences, 1840–1937; a union list of their publications available in libraries of the United States and Canada. Edited by Winifred Gregory under the auspices of the Bibliographical society of America.

Mathematics — queen of the sciences. Edited by Frieda Maurie Heller. (Reading for background.)

Key to the out-of-doors; a bibliography of nature books and materials. Compiled by Richard James Hurley.

My vocation, by eminent Americans; or, What eminent Americans think of their callings. Edited by Earl Granger Lockhart.

Peace and rearmament. Compiled by Julia Emily Johnsen. (Reference shelf.)

Poetry for high schools. Compiled by Amelia H. Munson. (Reading for background.)

Quotations for special occasions. Compiled by Maud Van Buren.

Representative American speeches: 1937–1938. Compiled by Albert Craig Baird. (Reference shelf.)

Spanish personal names; principles governing their formation and use which may be presented as a help for catalogers and bibliographers. By Charles Francis Gosnell.

The state sales tax. Compiled and edited by Egbert Ray Nichols, Marian Murray Nichols, and Egbert Ray Nichols, Jr. (Reference shelf.)

Subject headings in education; a systematic list for use in a dictionary catalog. By Clyde Elaine Pettus.

United States foreign policy; isolation or alliance. Compiled by Julia Emily Johnsen. (Reference shelf.)

University debaters' annual; constructive and rebuttal speeches delivered in debates of American colleges and universities during the college year 1937–1938. Edited by Edith M. Phelps.

World war, the great crusade; a bibliography of materials for atmosphere and background for pupils in junior high school. By Frances Fitzgerald. (Reading for background.)

1939

American neutrality problem. By Charles Franklin Phillips and Jasper Vanderbilt Garland. (Contemporary social problems discussion series.)

American Shakespearean criticism, 1607–1865. By Alfred Van Rensselaer Westfall.

Bibliography of costume. Compiled by Hilaire and Meyer Hiler. Edited by Helen Grant Cushing.

Bibliography of crime and criminal justice, 1932–1937. Compiled by Dorothy Campbell Culver.

Bibliography of speech education. Compiled by Lester Thonssen and Elizabeth Fatherson.

Bibliography of the Island of Guam. Edited by Charles Frederick Reid.

Book quotation crostics and other puzzles. By Alice Neptune Gale.

Capital punishment. Compiled by Julia Emily Johnsen. (Reference shelf.)

Chain stores and legislation. Compiled and edited by Daniel Bloomfield. (Reference shelf.)

Compounding in the English language. By Alice Morton Ball.

Debate index. Compiled by Edith May Phelps. (Reference shelf.)

Doctoral dissertations accepted by American universities. No. 6, 1938–1939. Edited by D. B. Gilchrist.

Europe: Versailles to Warsaw. By Ronald Stuart Kain. (Reference shelf.)

Guide to the encyclicals of the Roman pontiffs from Leo XIII to the present day (1878–1937). Compiled by Sister Mary Claudia Carlen.

Life with men and books. By Arthur Elmore Bostwick.

List of French prose fiction from 1700 to 1750. Compiled by Silas Paul Jones.

Metal projects index. Compiled by William J. Becker.

New York city yesterday, today and tomorrow. Compiled by Mary F. Brady and edited by Helen Sutton Carpenter. (Reading for background.)

Public housing in America. Compiled by Morris Bartel Schnapper. (Reference shelf.)

Pump-priming theory of government spending. Edited by Egbert Ray Nichols. (Reference shelf.)

Radio censorship. Compiled by Harrison Boyd Summers. (Reference shelf.)

Radio roads to reading; library book talks broadcast to girls and boys. Edited by Julia L. Sauer.

Railroad problem, with reference to government ownership. Compiled by Harrison Boyd Summers and Robert Edward Summers. (Reference shelf.)

A reference index to twelve thousand Spanish American authors; a guide to the literature of Spanish America. By Raymond Leonard Grismer. (Inter-American bibliographical and library association publications. Series III.)

Representative American speeches: 1938–1939. Compiled by Albert Craig Baird. (Reference shelf.)

A Richard Wagner dictionary. By Edward M. Terry.

United States and war. Compiled by Julia Emily Johnsen. (Reference shelf.)

United States foreign policy (supplement). Compiled by Julia Emily Johnsen. (Reference shelf.)

University debaters' annual; constructive and rebuttal speeches delivered in debates of American colleges and universities during the college year 1938–1939. Edited by Edith M. Phelps.

1940

Anthology of public speeches. Compiled by Mabel Platz.

Background readings for journalism. Compiled by Gunnar Horn. (Reading for background.)

Bibliographic classification (vol. 1). By Henry Evelyn Bliss.

Bibliography of Latin American folklore. Compiled by Ralph Steele Boggs. (Inter-American bibliographical and library association publications. Series I.)

Bibliography of swimming. Compiled by Frances Anderson Greenwood.

Census of medieval and renaissance manuscripts in the United States and Canada (vol. 2). By Seymour de Ricci.

Centralized school library. By Helen E. Rimkus.

Compulsory military training. Compiled by Julia Emily Johnsen. (Reference shelf.)

Doctoral dissertations accepted by American universities. No. 7, 1939–1940. Edited by E. A. Henry.

Early New York library of fiction. By George Gates Raddin, Jr.

Eastern public speaking conferences, 1940. Edited by Harold F. Harding.

High school forensics; an integrated program. By Arnold E. Melzer.

How to debate; a textbook for beginners. By Harrison Boyd Summers and Forest Livings Whan.

Increasing federal power. Compiled by Harrison Boyd Summers and Robert Edward Summers. (Reference shelf.)

International news and the press; communications, organization of news-gathering, international affairs and the foreign press; an annotated bibliography. Compiled by Ralph O. Nafziger.

Interstate trade barriers. Compiled by Julia Emily Johnsen. (Reference shelf.)

Know your library; lecture notes for film strip. By Mary A. Bennett and Mary R. Lingenfelter.

Library on the air. Compiled by Marie Duvernoy Loizeaux.

List of subject headings for books by and about the Negro. By Frances Lydia Yocom.

Living musicians. Edited by David Ewen.

Manual for the arrangement and description of archives. By Samuel Muller, Johan Adriaan Feith, and Robert Fruin.

National labor relations act; should it be amended? Compiled by Julia Emily Johnsen. (Reference shelf.)

Pages from the Gutenberg Bible of 42 lines; 25 facsimiles from the copy in the General theological seminary, New York. With an introduction and notes by O. W. Fuhrmann.

Planned economy. Compiled by Harrison Boyd Summers and Robert Edward Summers. (Reference shelf.)

Radio workshop plays. By James M. Morris.

The railroads; government ownership in practice. Compiled by Harrison Boyd Summers and Robert Edward Summers. (Reference shelf.)

Readings for Italian; a bibliography of materials for atmosphere and background for teachers and pupils in foreign language classes. Compiled by Lavinia Caprio La Manna. (Reading for background.)

Representative American speeches: 1939–1940. Compiled by Albert Craig Baird. (Reference shelf.)

Russian composers and musicians; a biographical dictionary. Compiled by Alexandria Vodarsky-Shiraeff.

School library service in the United States; an interpretative survey. By Henry L. Cecil and Willard Allison Heaps.

Student congress movement; with discussion on American neutrality. Edited by Lyman Spicer Judson. (Reference shelf.)

Survey of special collections in New Jersey libraries.

Trade unions and the anti-trust laws. Compiled by Julia Emily Johnsen. Reference shelf.)

University debaters' annual; constructive and rebuttal speeches delivered in debates of American colleges and universities during the college year 1939–1940. Edited by Edith M. Phelps.

Victory; how women won it, a centennial, 1840–1940. By the National American woman suffrage association.

Who was when? a dictionary of contemporaries. By Mariam Allen De Ford.

1941

American book collectors and collecting; from colonial times to the present. By Carl Leslie Cannon.

American mottoes and slogans. By George Earlie Shankle.

Audio-visual materials for junior and senior high school reading. By Katherine Eleanor Wheeling and Jane Anderson Hilson.

Bibliography; a beginner's guide to the making, evaluation and use of bibliographies. By Marion Villiers Higgins.

Bibliography of the Virgin Islands of the United States. Edited by Charles Frederick Reid.

Book and library plays for elementary and high school use (vol. 2). Edited by Edith May Phelps.

Debate index supplement. Compiled by Edith May Phelps. (Reference shelf.)

Doctoral dissertations accepted by American universities. No. 8, 1940–1941. Edited by E. A. Henry.

Federal regulation of labor unions. Compiled by Jasper Vanderbilt Garland. (Reference shelf.)

Film index, a bibliography. Vol. 1: The film as art. Compiled by workers of the writers' program of the Works project administration in the city of New York; sponsored by the Museum of modern art film library.

International federation of democracies. Compiled by Julia Emily Johnsen. (Reference shelf.)

Magazines for high schools; an evaluation of a hundred titles. By Laura Katherine Martin.

Monroe doctrine and the growth of western hemisphere solidarity. Compiled by Richard K. Showman and Lyman Spicer Judson. (Reference shelf.)

Oral interpretation of literature in American colleges and universities; a historical study of teaching methods. By Mary Margaret Robb.

Representative American speeches: 1940–1941. Compiled by Albert Craig Baird. (Reference shelf.)

Universal military service. Compiled by Robert Edward Summers and Harrison Boyd Summers. (Reference shelf.)

University debaters' annual; constructive and rebuttal speeches delivered in debates of American colleges and universities during the college year 1940–1941. Edited by Edith M. Phelps.

War and the Americas. By Jasper Vanderbilt Garland. (Contemporary social problems discussion series.)

Western hemisphere defense. Compiled by Egbert Ray Nichols. (Reference shelf.)

1942

Background readings on Latin America. Compiled by Sarah M. Galvan. (Reading for background.)

Birth certificates; a digest of the laws and regulations of the various states. By Earl Harrison Davis.

Book selection for secondary school libraries. By Willard Allison Heaps.

Cataloging manual for law libraries. By Elsie Basset.

Closed shop. Compiled by Julia Emily Johnsen. (Reference shelf.)

County library primer. By Mildred W. Sandoe.

Doctoral dissertations accepted by American universities. No. 9, 1941–1942. Edited by E. A. Henry.

"Eight points" of post-war world reorganization. Compiled by Julia Emily Johnsen. (Reference shelf.)

Federal price control. Compiled by Julia Emily Johnsen. (Reference shelf.)

Federal sales tax. Compiled by Egbert Ray Nichols. (Reference shelf.)

Gateways to American history; an annotated graded list of books for slow learners in junior high school. By Helen McCracken Carpenter.

Histories and historians of Hispanic America. By Alva Curtis Wilgus. (Inter-American bibliographical and library association publications. Series I.)

Index to children's poetry. Compiled by John Edmund Brewton and Sara Westbrook Brewton.

Once upon a time; children's stories retold for broadcasting. By Katherine Williams Watson.

Patients' library; a guide book for volunteer hospital library service. By Mary Frank Mason.

Permanent price control policy. Compiled by Julia Emily Johnsen. (Reference shelf.)

Plans for a post-war world. Compiled by Julia Emily Johnsen. (Reference shelf.)

Representative American speeches: 1941–1942. Compiled by Albert Craig Baird. (Reference shelf.)

Research guide on cooperative group farming; a research bibliography on rural cooperative production and cooperative communities. By Joseph W. Eaton and Saul M. Katz.

Selected readings in rhetoric and public speaking. Compiled by Lester Thonssen.

Twentieth century authors; a biographical dictionary of modern literature. Edited by Stanley Jasspon Kunitz and Howard Haycraft. (Authors series.)

University debaters' annual; constructive and rebuttal speeches delivered in debates of American colleges and universities during the college year 1941–1942. Edited by Edith M. Phelps.

Wages and prices. Compiled by Robert Edward Summers. (Reference shelf.)

Wartime censorship of press and radio. Compiled by Robert Edward Summers. (Reference shelf.)

1943

Course for the storyteller, an outline. By Ruth Budd Galbraith.

Doctoral dissertations accepted by American universities. No. 10, 1942–1943. Edited by E. A. Henry.

Independence for India? Compiled by Julia Emily Johnsen. (Reference shelf.)

Index to plays in collections; an author and title index to plays appearing in collections published between 1900 and 1942. By John Henry Ottemiller.

Know the south; books with southern background. Compiled by Azile Wofford. (Reading for background series.)

Pied piper broadcasts; radio plays for children. By Sylvia Newton Thorne and Marion Norris Gleason.

Reconstituting the League of nations. Compiled by Julia Emily Johnsen. (Reference shelf.)

Representative American speeches: 1942–1943. Compiled by Albert Craig Baird. (Reference shelf.)

University debaters' annual; constructive and rebuttal speeches delivered in debates of American colleges and universities during the college year 1942–1943. Edited by Edith M. Phelps.

Wage stabilization and inflation. Compiled by Julia Emily Johnsen. (Reference shelf.)

World peace plans. Compiled by Julia Emily Johnsen. (Reference shelf.)

1944

Administration of the college library. By Guy R. Lyle.

Basic English. Compiled by Julia Emily Johnsen. (Reference shelf.)

Canada and the western hemisphere. Compiled by Julia Emily Johnsen. (Reference shelf.)

Current abbreviations. By George Earlie Shankle.

Doctoral dissertations accepted by American universities. No. 11, 1943–1944. Edited by E. A. Henry.

Gateways to readable books; an annotated graded list of books in many fields for adolescents who find reading difficult. By Ruth Strang, Alice Checkovitz, Christine Gilbert, and Margaret Scoggin.

International police force. Compiled by Julia Emily Johnsen. (Reference shelf.)

Language of World War II. Compiled by Anna Marjorie Taylor.

Lowering the voting age. Compiled by Julia Emily Johnsen. (Reference shelf.)

Representative American speeches: 1943–1944. Compiled by Albert Craig Baird. (Reference shelf.)

R. B. library catalog. Compiled by the H. W. Wilson company.

Subject headings used in the dictionary catalogs of the Library of Congress. Cumulated supplements to the 4th edition, 1941–1943.

University debaters' annual; constructive and rebuttal speeches delivered in debates of American colleges and universities during the college year 1943–1944. Edited by Edith M. Phelps.

1945

Competitive debate; rules and strategy. By George McCoy Musgrave.

Compulsory arbitration of labor disputes. Compiled by Julia Emily Johnsen. (Reference shelf.)

Doctoral dissertations accepted by American universities. No. 12, 1944–1945. Edited by Arnold H. Trotier.

Dumbarton Oaks. Compiled by Robert Edward Summers. (Reference shelf.)

Encyclopedia of the Negro; preparatory volume with reference lists and reports. By William Edward Burghardt Du Bois and Guy Benton Johnson.

International airways. Compiled by Alberta Worthington. (Reference shelf.)

Makers of democracy in Latin America. By Harold Eugene Davis.

Peacetime conscription. Compiled by Julia Emily Johnsen. (Reference shelf.)

Postwar wage stabilization. Compiled by Julia Emily Johnsen. (Reference shelf.)

Representative American speeches: 1944–1945. Compiled by Albert Craig Baird. (Reference shelf.)

University debaters' annual; constructive and rebuttal speeches delivered in debates of American colleges and universities during the college year 1944–1945. Edited by Edith M. Phelps.

1946

American capitalism vs. Russian communism. Compiled by Clarence A. Peters. (Reference shelf.)

Anatomy of racial intolerance. Compiled by George Bernard de Huszar. (Reference shelf.)

Atomic bomb. Compiled by Julia Emily Johnsen. (Reference shelf.)

Cervantes: a bibliography. By Raymond Leonard Grismer.

Challenge: background readings for and about the physically handicapped, adults and children. Compiled by Agnes Shields and Marcia Hill. (Reading for background.)

Doctoral dissertations accepted by American universities. No. 13, 1945–1946. Edited by Arnold H. Trotier.

Free medical care. Compiled by Clarence A. Peters. (Reference shelf.)

International trade: cooperative or competitive? Compiled by Clarence A. Peters. (Reference shelf.)

Juvenile delinquency: a critical annotated bibliography. Compiled by Philippe Sidney de Q. Cabot.

Occupations; a selected list of pamphlets. By Gertrude Forrester.

Palestine: Jewish homeland? Compiled by Julia Emily Johnsen. (Reference shelf.)

Representative American speeches: 1945–1946. Compiled by Albert Craig Baird. (Reference shelf.)

Subject headings; the history and theory of the alphabetical subject approach to books. By Julia Ensign Pettee.

University debaters' annual; constructive and rebuttal speeches delivered in debates of American colleges and universities during the college year 1945–1946. Edited by Edith M. Phelps.

1947

Bibliographic classification (vol. 2). By Henry Evelyn Bliss.

Compulsory federal arbitration of labor disputes. Compiled by Julia Emily Johnsen. (Reference shelf.)

Doctoral dissertations accepted by American universities. No. 14, 1946–1947. Edited by Arnold H. Trotier.

Extempore speaking: a handbook for the student, the coach, and the judge. By Donald L. Holley.

Flowers of prairie and woodland. By Edith Schwartz Clements.

Metropolitan opera annals. Compiled by William H. Seltsam, with an introduction by Edward Johnson. Sponsored by the Metropolitan opera guild, inc.

Radio plays for children. Compiled by Katherine Williams Watson.

Representative American speeches: 1946–1947. Compiled by Albert Craig Baird. (Reference shelf.)

United nations or world government? Compiled by Julia Emily Johnsen. (Reference shelf.)

University debaters' annual; constructive and rebuttal speeches delivered in debates of American colleges and universities during the college year 1946–1947. Edited by Edith M. Phelps and Ruth Ulman.

1948

America, past and present. Compiled by Eloise Rue and others. (Reading for background series.)

Best books of the decade, 1936–1945. Compiled by Asa Don Dickinson.

Dilemma of postwar Germany. Compiled by Julia Emily Johnsen. (Reference shelf.)

Doctoral dissertations accepted by American universities. No. 15, 1947–1948. Edited by Arnold H. Trotier.

Economic aid to Europe: the Marshall plan. Compiled by Robert Edward Summers. (Reference shelf.)

Federal world government. Compiled by Julia Emily Johnsen. (Reference shelf.)

Immigration problem. Compiled by Clarence A. Peters. (Reference shelf.)

Index to reproductions of American paintings; a guide to pictures occuring in more than eight hundred books. Compiled by Isabel Stevenson Monro and Kate Margaret Monro.

A job for every woman. By Louise Morgenstern Neuschutz.

Library broadcasts. By Frances G. Nunmaker.

Occupational pamphlets; an annotated bibliography. By Gertrude Forrester.

Representative American speeches: 1947–1948. Compiled by Albert Craig Baird. (Reference shelf.)

Teaching through the elementary school library. By Margaret Kessler Walraven and Alfred L. Hall-Quest.

University debaters' annual; constructive and rebuttal speeches delivered in debates of American colleges and universities during the college year 1947–1948. Edited by Ruth Ulman.

1949

American composers today; a biographical and critical guide. Compiled and edited by David Ewen.

Democracy through discussion. By Bruno Lasker.

Direct election of the President. Compiled by Julia Emily Johnsen. (Reference shelf.)

Doctoral dissertations accepted by American universities. No. 16, 1948–1949. Edited by Arnold H. Trotier.

Dynamics of vegetation; selections from the writings of Frederic Edward Clements. Compiled and edited by B. W. Allred and Edith Schwartz Clements.

Equality in America: the issue of minority rights. Compiled by George Bernard de Huszar. (Reference shelf.)

Federal information controls in peacetime. Compiled by Robert Edward Summers. (Reference shelf.)

Index to composers and list of errata discovered in the first printing of Metropolitan opera annals. Compiled by William H. Seltsam.

Inflation: causes and cures. Compiled by Thomas O. Waage. (Reference shelf.)

Latin American leaders. By Harold Eugene Davis.

Representative American speeches: 1948–1949. Compiled by Albert Craig Baird. (Reference shelf.)

Should the Communist party be outlawed? Compiled by Julia Emily Johnsen. (Reference shelf.)

University debaters' annual; constructive and rebuttal speeches delivered in debates of American colleges and universities during the college year 1948–1949. Edited by Ruth Ulman.

A Note on Sources

Most of the material for this book has been collected over a period of several months from the archives of the company and in interviews with members of the staff.

Mr. Wilson has been extremely generous with his time, proving an expert guide on this exploration of the past. He has been the principal and, in fact, the only adequate source of information about his childhood and youth. He has enriched the report by frequent revelations — sometimes by straight exposition, sometimes by an anecdote — of the philosophy of service which has motivated his lifework. His personal files have been a rich treasure; and some of these pages, indeed, could not have been written without them. The company's critics have always prefaced their arguments with a confession of their admiration for Mr. Wilson's integrity and candor in answering their inquiries. The writer now knows from experience that such praise was more than mere courtesy.

Some of the most valuable information was extracted from a massive collection of leaflets and brochures published by the company during the last four or five decades. These promotion folders were largely written by Edith M. Phelps, the retired secretary of the company, who spent a day with the writer rummaging through them, explaining points in them that time had obscured, and elaborating on past events suggested by them.

The documents have been supplemented by the spoken word.

Of those who graciously submitted to being cross-examined for hours on end, Marion E. Potter should head the list. From her well-stocked memory, she supplied many of the personal and humorous details which, one hopes, have enlivened parts of this otherwise sober chronicle.

Others must be briefly mentioned. The writer gratefully acknowledges the aid of the following executives: Howard Haycraft, vice president of the company; Charles J. Shaw, assistant to the president; John C. Evans, advertising manager; Arthur Rigg, head of the accounting department; E. O. Erickson, director of the Periodicals Clearing House; and Edward S. Kelley, superintendent of the printing and binding departments.

The following editorial personnel deserve recognition for patient acceptance of what must have been at times a serious interruption in their crowded working day: John Jamieson, editor of General Publications; Regina Goldman, editor of the *Cumulative Book Index*; Dorothy E. Cook and Dorothy West, editors of the *Standard Catalog Series*; Sarita Robinson, editor of the *Readers' Guide to Periodical Literature*; Bea Joseph, editor of *Biography Index*; Beatrice Rakestraw, editor of *Art Index*; Florence D. Phin, editor of the *Vertical File Service*; Anne Rothe, editor of *Current Biography*; Mertice James and Dorothy Brown, editors of the *Book Review Digest*; Dorothy Carpenter, editor of *Education Index*; Florence Arnold, editor of *Agricultural Index*; Dorothy Cole, editor of *Library Literature*; Virginia Turrell, editor of *Bibliographic Index*; Dorothy Charles, editor of *International Index*; Marie D. Loizeaux, editor of the *Wilson Library Bulletin*; and Ethel Ashworth, chief of the Production Department.

The writer is also indebted to several former employees — Mary K. Reely, Lucie Wallace, Marion Knight, Lillian Henley, Mary Burnham, Marian Shaw, Mrs. Sydney Crawford, Edward G. Perine, and Charles R. Brockmann — for their letters in reply to his appeal for assistance.

Certain magazine articles and booklets have been useful:

Creighton Peet. "A Mousetrap in the Bronx." *New Yorker*, vol. 14, no. 37 (Oct. 29, 1938). (Profile of Mr. Wilson.)

Edith M. Phelps. "Forty Years of Debate Publishing." *Quarterly Journal of Speech*, vol. 34, no. 2 (April 1948), pp. 162–67.

H. W. Wilson Co. *Current Biography*, vol. 9, no. 5 (May 1948), pp. 58–60. (Sketch of Mr. Wilson.)

H. W. Wilson Co. *A Quarter Century of Cumulative Bibliography*. New York, 1923. 44p.

H. W. Wilson Co. *Wilson Library Bulletin*, vol. 22, no. 10 (June 1948). (Anniversary issue.)

H. W. Wilson Co. *The Daily Cumulative*. June 22–27, 1908. (Published during the American Library Association meeting in Minneapolis.)

H. W. Wilson Co. *Among Ourselves*. Minneapolis, v.d. (House organ.)

The University of Minnesota background has been derived from various issues (1895–1898) of the *Minnesota Magazine*; the *Gopher*, senior class annual; and the *Ariel*, student weekly newspaper. The writer has also consulted Oscar Firkins' *Cyrus Northrop: A Memoir* (Minneapolis, University of Minnesota Press, 1925; 634p); Helen Whitney's *Maria Sanford* (Minneapolis, 1922; 322p); and Theodore C. Blegen's "A State University Is Born," pp. 151–95 in *The Land Lies Open* (Minneapolis, University of Minnesota Press, 1949; 246p).

The sections devoted to the history of bibliographic publishing are based on scattered numbers of the *Library Journal* and on the following books and pamphlets:

ADOLF GROWOLL. "Three Centuries of English Book Trade Bibliography; An Essay on the Progress of Book Trade Bibliography since the Introduction of Printing and in England since 1595 . . ." New York Dibdin Club, 1903. 195p.

ADOLF GROWOLL. "Book-trade Bibliography in the United States in the 19th Century . . ." New York Dibdin Club, 1898. 79p. (Parts of this book appeared in *Publishers' Weekly*, June 12, 19, and 26, and July 3, 1897.)

TORSTEIN JAHR and A. J. STROHM. "Bibliography of Cooperative Cataloguing and the Printing of Catalogue Cards . . . (1850–1902)." Washington, Government Printing Office, 1903. 116p. (Reprinted from the Report of the Librarian of Congress.)

WILLIAM FREDERICK POOLE. *Library Journal*, vol. 3, no. 5 (July 1878). (Autobiographical sketch.)

PUBLISHERS' WEEKLY. *Descriptive List of the Bibliographic Publications Issued by the Office of "The Publishers' Weekly."* New York, 1903. 20p.

HALSEY WILLIAM WILSON. *The Bookman's Reading and Tools.* New York, H. W. Wilson Co., 1932. 62p.

H. W. WILSON Co. "Indexes to General Periodicals." *Readers' Guide Supplement*, vol. 1, no. 1 (March 1931).

H. W. WILSON Co. "Subject vs. Title Indexes." Minneapolis, n.d. (Promotion circular reprinting early arguments from the *Library Journal*.)

H. W. WILSON Co. "Announcement of Important Changes in the Plan of Publication of the *Cumulative Book Index* and the *Publishers' Weekly* . . ." Minneapolis, December 1, 1911. 4p.

H. W. WILSON Co. "Cooperation and the *Readers' Guide to Periodical Literature*: Support of Bibliographical Publications." Minneapolis, n.d. 8p.

The discussion of the service basis resulted from lengthy conversations with Mr. Wilson, Mr. Haycraft, and other members of the firm. It has also followed a study of numerous company statements and these typewritten or mimeographed reports (listed in chronological order):

MILES O. and FANNIE E. PRICE. "The 'Service Basis' Methods of Pricing Certain Books and Periodical Indexes: a Preliminary Statistical Study of Some of its Economic Aspects." 1938. 152p (with appendices).

H. T. LEWIS, E. P. LEARNED, and S. F. TEELE. "Commentary on the Study of the Wilson Company's Pricing Policy and Methods made by Mr. and Mrs. Price." 1940. 4p.

M. LLEWELLYN RANEY and HAROLD L. LEUPP. "The H. W. Wilson Company's System of Scale Pricing: a Critical and Constructive Examination." 1941. 61p.

H. W. WILSON Co. "The Service Basis of Charge: Reply to 'A Critical and Constructive Examination' by Raney and Leupp." December 24, 1941. 15p.

CHARLES W. DAVID. "Report to the Committee on Indexing and Abstracting, American Library Association." February 10, 1944. 23p. (Includes letter, Feb. 11, 1944, from Edith M. Phelps to Mr. David, answering several questions in regard to the policy.)

KIRK P. DRAHEIM and EDWARD N. WRIGHT. "Analysis of Cost Elements Involved in the H. W. Wilson Pricing Policy." 1943. 4p.

H. W. WILSON Co. "Reply to the Draheim-Wright Report." October 22, 1943. 3p.

STANLEY F. TEELE. "The H. W. Wilson Company." April 2, 1945. 2p. (Report to K. D. Metcalf, Harvard University, Member of the Committee on Indexing and Abstracting, American Library Association.)

The sections on financing and labor relations are based on interviews with Mr. Rigg, Mr. Shaw, and Leone Baker, president of the H. W. Wilson Company Employees Association. Also examined were the company's articles of incorporation, dated December 26, 1913; a letter from Warren C. Rowell to the employees dated January 1, 1918; and the contract negotiated in 1949 by the company and its employees.

For general library matters, the writer has relied upon the *Guide to the Use of Libraries* by Margaret Hutchins, Alice Johnson, and Margaret Williams (5th ed., 1938, 252p) and *The Library Key* by Zaidee Brown (6th ed., 1946, 147p) — both published by the Wilson company. James Howard Wellard's *The Public Library Comes of Age* (London, 1940, 204p) has also been highly useful.

It should be repeated, however, that the primary sources have been the firm's enormous files of correspondence, numberless circulation pamphlets, the *Wilson Library Bulletin*, and the catalogs and indexes themselves, which occasionally contain prefaces of historical interest.

But, above all, the writer is grateful to the present members of the staff for their unfailing kindness.

Index